WELCOME TO A

RICH PUBLICATIONS

PRESENTATION

FEATURING RICH GILMORE

I

DIVAGIRL

"Having A Good Man Find You
While
Maximizing Your Womanhood In The Process"

RICH GILMORE

RICH PUBLICATIONS LLC

Published by
RICH PUBLICATIONS
P.O. Box 118
Lyndhurst, NJ 07071

www.richpublications.com

ISBN: 0-9746834-2-6
TXu1-145-563

Written by Rich Gilmore
Edited by Tanisha Gilmore
Cover design created by Rich Gilmore and Roland Hall

<u>Special Thanks</u>

I thank God for the Spirit, the Gift, and the Assignment,

Thanks to my wife and life partner Tanisha for holding your man down like a real Diva. Thanks for being a good thing for me and to me...Luv Ya Lil Mama,

To my right hand Tom a.k.a "T- Boogz" thanks for being in the pit and working the grind like a soldier... Let's get it my nucker.....

To my mother Adrienne, my sisters Kenya and Niya, my nieces Keniya, Meadow, and Raven...luv y'all

I would like to send a special thanks to every African American writer, artist, thinker, business great, and publisher past and present, for paving the way and for opening the doors that I run through. I will continue to move us forward raising the bar as I go.

SPECIAL BIG THANKS

TO YOU

THE READER....

Other Hot Books by Rich Gilmore

Real Book Series Chapter I
Punaney Galore
"The Sexiest Story Ever Told"

Real Book Series Chapter II
Real Men Do Real Things
"How Real Men Get Down."

Rich Living Series Volume I
Money Laws of The Baller Shot Caller

Coming Soon (2005)

Real Book Series Chapter III
Sex, Money, Drugs, & Consequence
"The Realist Story Ever Told"

To view our entire catalog
Visit Rich Gilmore and RICH PUBLICATIONS at:
www. RichPublications.com
OR
**Visit Your Local Borders, Waldens, and Neighborhood
Bookstore To Purchase More Rich Gilmore Titles**

CONTENTS

Special Message

This is a Divine Appointment between who you are today as a woman and your very best possible as the feminine manifestation of God. The fact that Divagirl is currently in your possession reveals that you have been pre-ordained to prosper, succeed, and to enjoy a life of satisfaction in this lifetime. The words in this book are Spirit, but the message of Divagirl unfolds in a very practical, everyday way.

If at the moment you are alittle apprehensive about taking this journey because you're thinking it's another one of "those books", if you're thinking "ain't no men out here, they are all living on the D-Low", or if you're growing tired of today's man, realize that everything happens for a reason and in an appointed season. And this message of Divagirl is for you to become more as a woman, to acccomplish more as a woman, and to possess more love and happiness in your world: And your season is *NOW*. Now is your time to be happy... now is your time to experience love like never before... now is your time to step into the phenomenal woman that you truly are.

So open up your heart and soul and let Divagirl take you to a new place and higher level......................

Rich Gilmore

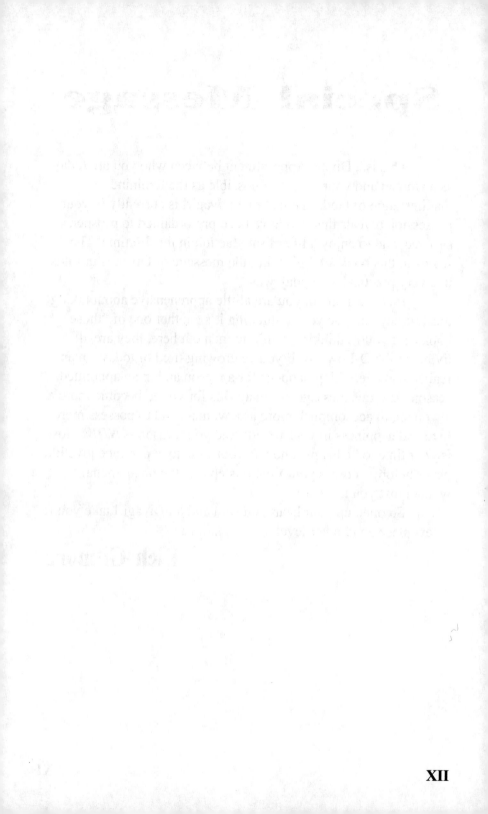

INTRODUCTION

"My message and my preaching were not with wise and persuasive words but with a demonstration of the Spirit's power, so that your faith might not rest on men's wisdom, but on God's power." (1Corinthians 2:4-5 NIV)

I want to get something clear right from the very first line in this book. There is no other book on the entire market like this one. If you picked up this book because it had a nice title and you thought it would contain the same contents as Honey, Cosmopolitan, or any other women's magazine or book you have read, or currently read... you're **WRONG!**

If you purchased this book thinking you were going to learn some more "silly" ass dating schemes, you're terribly mistaken. If you think that just by reading this book a good man will walk into your life and sweep you off of your feet, then I'm sorry to inform you; but you're delusional babygirl.

This is not any make believe Fantasy Island "say whatever sounds good to sell books" stuff. This is the hardcore truth. If you picked up this book because you are willing to become more as a woman, then this book is for you. If you picked up this book because you are dissatisfied with your relationships with men and you want to make some changes, then you made a great move with this purchase.

If you are courageous enough to look in the mirror and stop the finger pointing, then this book will change your life for the better. This book wasn't written to celebrate your pain as a woman, but to increase your prosperity. This book wasn't created to bash men and elevate the women. This book was written so that we can understand one another and live in love.

I'm telling you right from jump, this won't be an Michael Baisden, TD Jakes, or Iyanla Vanzant experience (I have nothing but respect for those individual's efforts). This is hardcore and real. This is that good ole "common sense" slap you in the face, principle centered truth.

This book is all about positive change, greater possibilities, and realizing your highest potential as a woman. There are far too many women thinking they are second class citizens on planet earth because of historical social conditioning (brainwashing). So I want for us to get back to exactly who you are as a woman.

This book is about bringing the truth back into your "reality". It's about walking in all the power, purpose, and prosperity that you are entitled to as a woman and creation of God.

This book is about getting right as a woman, in order that Mr. Right will recognize you. If you will open up your heart and soul, the principles in this book will take you to another level as a woman. If you open up, this book will greatly enhance your relationship with men. Trust me, you are gonna be happy that you made this purchase. **I GUARANTEE IT!**

I write to you not as some self-proclaimed guru, expert on relationships, or as some Ph.D. from NYU. Not even for one second am I claiming to have all the answers. That would only be displaying my ignorance. I know that the more we learn, the more our ignorance is exposed. So don't expect me to tell you what you "should" do with your life. This is not that type of book. Besides none of that "should" advice works anyway.

I'm speaking on behalf of the single, heterosexual man in America. I'm a regular everyday brother that you might bump into at the club, on line in the grocery store, or see in church (every once in a while). I come with a message of power and principle for all of you ladies, regardless of your walk in life. I'm telling you, I have something special in store for you babygirl.

I first have to warn you. This book is *off the hook*. I refuse to sugarcoat or cheat you out of what I believe God has placed on my heart to give. I will lay it all on the line, the good, the bad, and the ugly. I plan on dealing with many of the common mentalities, lifestyles, and situations that we find ourselves in during a relationship. I will share with you the fundamental mentality of men today and reveal to you how we, as *men*, really get down. I'm gonna put you on to why we do what we do. I will also be sharing with you some fundamental principles of womanhood and effective living that will take your life to higher levels. So expect to be uplifted and empowered.

I also plan on giving you that which is too explicit for magazine and not politically correct enough for television. So if you're very sensitive with an extremely low level of self-esteem, this book might be a little too much for you babydoll. If you're used to being the *victim* and want me to support your pain; move on to another book. I'm not trying to be an asshole and I'm definitely not trying to be insensitive (that's not my MO), but there will be times throughout this book where you may think so. I just propose that you hear me out and listen for the real message to what I'm saying before you start sending the hate mail (ha, ha).

This book will cause you to do many things. You're going to think, laugh, shake your head in agreement, have profound moments. You're gonna want to call your girl Pam, slap your mama and dem`, and you're gonna want to curse me out. You are gonna forgive people, learn new things about yourself, feel good and accept yourself in a new way, realize how blessed you are, and come to appreciate the male creation like never before. I'm telling you babygirl this book is a "fulfilling" experience. Trust me, I'm gonna be hitting you from every angle, getting real deep in your insides. (Sounds good right booboo)

We are going to have a "real" time throughout this book. So get comfortable and get excited. I have some of that good stuff for you Ms. Lady. I don't have any religious affiliation nor do I have some "stiff" reputation to uphold. Therefore, we can talk like we are alone somewhere on a white sand beach, with some Luther Vandross playing, as we sip on some Bahamamamas.

Seriously speaking, the language, the grammar, and all of the other things people are conscious of when "trying" to make a good impression on someone, I really don't care about. I'm not trying to impress you. I just want to talk to you. In fact, I would like to look at this as more of a conversation, than as a book. So relax and enjoy the experience for what it is.

If you happen to disagree with me or feel offended by what I share, that's perfectly okay with me. I write every word in a Spirit of love, with my conscience clear and pure. Therefore, I'm free of fear, worry, and the opinion of man. I'm quite sure that you will be enlightened, educated, and entertained throughout this book. So let's get to it already.

GET READY

Now I'm gonna need you to do me a simple favor before we get started. I don't care where you may be right now, I need you to close your eyes for thirty seconds, take three deep breaths, and just relax yourself.

I know that for some of you, relaxing is the hardest thing in the world to do…But do it anyway. Okay... that's it. That was all I needed you to do for me.

Now if you didn't take the time to relax, go ahead and do so now. I'll wait for you to finish… See how good that makes you feel. It's a shame that the only time many of you ladies feel relaxed is after some good sex. Tragically, many of you aren't getting that as often as you would like. (It's a damn shame)

It's imperative that you are in a calm state while reading this book. You are gonna have to look deep within yourself at times. You may have to deal with some things that lay buried deep down in your subconscious mind. I'm talking about the "stuff" (attitudes, feelings, beliefs) that you don't consciously recognize is directing your life. So if you have to, go into another room. Leave the kids in their room to play by themselves.

Go into your bedroom and leave your husband or babyfather to himself. Let him sit in the living room, watching TV, and scratching his balls. If you are single and live alone, go put on some soft music, turn the telephone ringer and the TV off. Do whatever you have to do to create a peaceful atmosphere for me and you. Just a reminder, if you do have little children, wait until they are asleep before you get your read on. (Always do the mommy thing first)

I hope by now, I was able to get you to relax, because now it's time to get it on like Marvin Gaye.

The key to getting answers in life is to ask your life some questions. So naturally, I'm going to ask you many questions throughout the book. I do so, so that you can find the answers you've been looking for all along.

All the questions I ask in this book are for you to answer for *yourself*... because they are *your answers* (get it). What good is it, if I give you all the answers to your life questions, and I don't even know you and your experience? That is why I don't have any "silly ass" dating schemes, telling you when to call, kiss, or when to sleep with a man.

My intentions are to treat you like a grown ass woman and I respect your right of choice and judgements. I will however challenge your decision making, if need be, and provide you with some more productive options to choose from. My goal is to help you get to the point where you realize your answers in life lay deep within yourself. My goal is to get you to the point where you value and trust yourself as a woman. I want to help you live the life you choose to live without regret and full of wisdom. I want you full of confidence, okay sexy lady.

The truth is, the answers to your life's questions are stashed underneath your fears, false beliefs, and ego. That's why I will do whatever I need to do, to strip you of all those deadly things. I want you to live and shine brightly, having men falling all over themselves as they try to get next to you. Trust me, it won't matter if you're overweight, short, tall, slim, black, white, or yellow. Once we are finished you will be more woman than you are right now.
I PROMISE!

So now I'm gonna need you to answer three simple questions for me:

DivaGirl - How To Have A Good Man Find You

QUESTIONS:

     1. Do you feel that you're all of the woman you can be right now?

     2. Are you honestly willing to correct your "wrongs", to get things "right"?

     3. What is your definition and characteristics of a "good man"?

     Take the time and answer those questions. The answers to those questions are the foundation you are standing on right now. Your answers to those questions will also determine where you are mentally. So honestly answer those questions. It's only to your benefit that you do so.

     In fact, go and get two or three separate sheets of paper right now. Use them to record all of your answers throughout the book. It's important that you write down your answers instead of just think about them. That way, you can monitor your development throughout the process. Believe me you will **_GROW_**.

     So here we are. I hope you are a little bit more comfortable and excited about what we are getting into. I know I'm excited about you purchasing this book to read. It shows we have made a valuable connection. You have just added value to my life with your purchase (I need to pay these damn bills) ha, ha. So let me add value to your life with my words. It's a beautiful thing we have going on, you would have to agree. So now that we know what's going on, let's go and get it on… for real this time…

CHAPTER 1

ALL MEN ARE GOOD!

"So God created man in his own image, in the image of God he created him, male and female he created them... God saw all that he had made and it was very good."

(Genesis 1:27, 31 NIV)

INTRODUCTION

Now I'm going to be straight up with you. This chapter might disturb the hell out of you. Good, that's exactly what I want to do. I want to disturb the *hell* out of you. When I say "hell", I mean those false things that separate you from experiencing your heaven on earth.

Like I mentioned earlier in the introduction, I'm going after everything that's false. I want you to see through many of the lies that you have been taught to believe in. My only objective is sharing and seeking truth, nothing more, nothing less. I want to see you walking in the fullness of your womanhood, with a good man by your side.

I have to warn you dear lady. This chapter is going to address and deal with some deep seated issues that might reside in the private parts of you.

This chapter is a little technical and extremely spiritual in nature. It's the foundation this whole book will rest on. I will say this: If you can honestly handle this chapter, then you are on your way to realizing more peace, happiness, and success in your life. This chapter is essential to all that we will cover throughout this book. Once again I have to warn you: This chapter is extremely spiritual in nature. Don't get it twisted, we will play a lot throughout the book. We first need to think and lay down a foundation. So read to understand not just to be entertained. If the chapter is a little too technical for you...move on to the next one. But whatever you do, don't stop reading the book.

God's Image

"God is a dog", "God ain't shit", "You can't trust God". How does all of that sound to you? I can just feel many of you are ready to close the book and return it to the store, because of what I just said.

Now let me ask you how do this sound? "Men are dogs", "Men ain't shit", "You can't trust no man". Obviously the first set of quotes sound like blaspheme, while the second set of quotes sound practical and true. I'm here to tell you. Both sets of quotes are false, wrong, and blasphemous.

I have to be clear about something, all of which that I am about to conclude in this chapter is predicated on my belief in the Bible as being the principled truth in the earth and the Word of God.

So like I said earlier, you are entitled to disagree with me. But at least hear me out. I'm not a preachy type of dude but I am very principled. So just let me do what I do. I will always lay down a foundation before I build a case. So follow me babygirl,

If it's not right and blasphemous to say that, "God ain't shit", but okay for you to say that, "Men ain't shit", and God made man in his image. What are we really saying? When you look in a mirror you see your image, right? So if that were true, what would happen if God were to look in a mirror? What would he see? His image of course.

Now don't get too literal on me. Don't sit there trying to figure out, how would God look at himself in a mirror. **STAY FOCUSED**.

If God made man in his image, man must look like God, right? Therefore, if you're saying, "men are dogs", or that "men ain't shit". What are you saying about God? Think about that for a minute. What are you really saying about God?

When you look in a mirror, aren't your expectations to see a clear image of yourself? Now what would you think, if you looked into your bathroom mirror and saw Sealy from the Color Purple looking back at you? It would trip you out of course. You would probably run right out of the bathroom into a plastic surgeon's chair to get chopped up?

Obviously, you would think something was wrong with your mirror, if when you looked in it you didn't see yourself. You might even think that someone was playing a trick on you, right? Now my next question is, if "men ain't shit", then who are you looking at? If "men are dogs", then what are you looking at? If "you can't trust a man", then who are you listening to? Obviously, something is wrong with your mirror.

To my knowledge, God only made one type of man. To my knowledge, the man that God made was created in a godly image and likeness that all was "good". According to my mirror, all the men I see are good. So what happened to you? What's going on with your look? I think someone has been playing a trick on you?

Is the mirror you're looking at real or false? Is it clear or distorted? I tell you, unless you are seeing "men as good", then your mirror is all the way wrong babydoll. I'm here to tell you, if all men ain't good, then you've been hoodwinked, bamboozled, and lead astray. The good news is, I'm here to help you get the proper mirror. I'm gonna help you get the right look and perspective.

Today we live in a culture and climate where we call men everything but "good". There may be a few separate instances where you ladies may classify an individual as a "good man". However, collectively men and manhood is viewed as a negative thing in the eyes of many, especially in the eyes of you women. For those of you that grew up in an abusive, unloving, or manless household, it might seem impossible for you right now to accept this truth. If a man has caused you pain, neglected your cries, or didn't respect your desires and position as a woman, I understand that what I'm saying may seem ludicrous to you. But listen to me anyway.

If your biological father abandoned you or if your babyfather is an asshole, I understand how difficult this may be for you to digest as truth. Trust me, I know that you might not be trying to hear this right now.

I hope you do realize that the truth doesn't need your approval before it becomes true. I know your ego will have you thinking that the sun rises and sets on your ass. But that's not really what time it is out here. Here's an example:

Let's say you and I go on a vacation to the Caribbean Islands. While on the trip, we decide to go skinny dipping. Now before we get into that crystal clear ocean water, I tell you that the water is twelve feet deep. Now for some reason you don't *believe* that what I'm telling you is *true*. What would happen if you jumped your naked ass in that water, not believing what I said was true and you couldn't swim? That's right, it would be a wrap for you. You would drown in that water because of your unbelief.

See the truth never has to be proven, it only has to be accepted on our part. The truth is one of the few elements in life that isn't subject to change or looking to prove itself. The truth is free. It just exists in eternity.

Therefore, if it's true that man is made in God's image and God is a good God. Then man must be a "good man". Remember, the truth doesn't have to be proven but accepted. I will however give you some principles. I want to make things clearer for you to understand and easier for you to accept.

Just keep in mind; I'm not trying to prove anything to you. This is something that you have to *accept* and live with.

DivaGirl - How To Have A Good Man Find You

Fact, Opinions, & Situations

Do you know the difference between a fact and an opinion? Do you really know the difference between a situation and a possibility? For the most part, I would say you do know the difference once you really think about it. My next question is, how many of us really think about it?

How often do you catch yourself reacting or treating your opinion about something as a fact? How often are you in a heated debate and damn near fistfight with someone trying to prove your point (opinion)?

Have you ever made an opinion about someone or something by the first impression, and then had a totally different opinion about the same person or thing later on? Of course you did. Remember when you first thought, "Michael was ugly"? But then you found out what he did for a living, and saw that luxury car he drove. Then Michael miraculously became "sexy". Remember how all of that made him "attractive" all of a sudden? (You remember)

I know it's a dirty game we play, but we are all guilty of it. It happens all day everyday. We walk around with a million different opinions about everything, with little to no facts about something, and think we are right about all things. We think we know the truth.

It's disgusting when you really think about it, because all opinions are subject to change. But for some reason we act like they are concrete and true, because they are *our opinions*.

The truth, however always remain the same. Whether something was true two thousand years ago or true yesterday, it's still true today. It's important that you record your answers to certain questions. You will see just how many of your beliefs are nothing but opinions. Therefore, they will change with exposure and experience.

Even if all of your beliefs are facts, all facts are subject to change as well. So understand how much room there is for change and growth in your life. Be excited, because you can drastically change your situations with the truth.

Currently, it might be a fact that the man who impregnated your mother wasn't much of a father to you. In your opinion right now, all men might be "dogs". You may currently find yourself in an unhealthy situation and relationship with a man. But that is all subject to change. The truth of the matter is, "all men are good", regardless of your opinions, the facts in your life, and your situations.

The purpose of this book is to help you manifest the truth into your attitudes and conversation. That way, your situations will line up with the "good life" God created for you to have. Keep in mind one of the objectives in this book is to have a good man find you.

In the introduction, I asked for your definition of a "good man". I'm quite sure that by the end of this book your definition will have changed drastically. Therefore, it's critical that you have written your answer down. It's the measuring stick we will use to gauge your progress.

I plan on bringing your answers into the mirror of truth. Just remember I want us to see what's really good.
"All men are good!"

God's Truth Vs Public Opinion

We are living in the most opinionated and confused time in history. There are messages being communicated to you all day long. Everyday, we are bombarded with information and images that seek to become experience in our lives.

Corporations invest large sums of money into advertisement campaigns, in hopes of getting you to think and act a certain way. They want you to think they have your best interest at heart and obviously they want you to buy their product or service.... It's just business babygirl.

Your family members and friends are always giving their

opinions, in hopes of convincing you that their thinking is right. They want you to take the advice they give.... It's all love though sweetheart.

Religions preach and teach their way to God, in order to have followers support their doctrine and dogma. They need to fill up their churches, synagogues, and temples.... It's all politics babydoll.

Everywhere you turn, it doesn't matter who you are, or where you are, there is an opinion about something you should be thinking, about something you should have in your possessions, about something you should be doing with your life, and an opinion about someone you should be.

In a society with so many opinions, interpretations, and perspectives, is it any wonder why there is so much conflict and confusion that exist? It's important now more so than ever before that we seek truth and not just accept what's popular or common if we want to experience peace of mind and freedom in our life.

If currently, you are dissatisfied with how your relationships with men have been manifesting then maybe your opinions, interpretations, and perspective are unsatisfactory. Maybe it's not the men? Maybe it's your thinking and doing that is bringing so much frustration to your life.

Many times in life when we are not happy with the results we're producing, we usually do one of two things: We *quit* or we *work harder*. Meaning exert more effort.

Quit

That's why some women have given up on men all together. Some of you ladies have just quit. You have just shut down and completely turned off your femininity and emotions towards men (It's a tragedy). As a result, your soul is damaged and you hurt deep down inside. You have to admit, it's hard being so cold and hard. Especially, when a big part of you wants to be held and supported.

DivaGirl - How To Have A Good Man Find You

Some women have turned to other women, looking for the love and strength of a man. Many do so, mainly out of frustration and pain. Some just take an "I don't care anymore" attitude. An attitude that often leads to mental, emotional, and physical ruin.

Work Harder

The other options many women choose when they are dissatisfied with the results they produce with men, is to work harder at the relationship. They will bend over backwards, accepting and conforming to anything, just to make that relationship work. They will do damn near anything just to get a man to notice and choose them.

Some women will date a married man, remain faithful to an abusive chump, and stay in an unhealthy relationship, as they work to make it work.

Logically, it appears to be a stupid thing to do. Some may even say or think that the woman is dumb and weak for doing what she does. The truth is, there is a lot of personal investment in the attitudes and beliefs that molds us. So no one understands how much of that woman has been invested into making her relationship work.

Have you noticed that a majority of our energy is used trying to prove and protect our opinions? Do you realize people go to war and kill for the protection of their opinions (beliefs)? Unfortunately, when many of you ladies are unhappy in a relationship with a man you don't consider a third alternative. You never consider that there may be something else that you can do. When you are unhappy or dissatisfied with a relationship, you can *change your opinions and attitudes about that man and relationship.*

Many times, we quit or work harder when that really isn't what we need to do. Often times, a new belief (opinion) is all we need in order to produce a new result. Keep in mind, it's the beliefs and attitudes we hold that determine our feelings and actions anyway. So by addressing our beliefs (opinions) first, we stand a better chance of being more effective in getting what we want.

It's also important to keep in mind that no matter how strong you may feel, or how long you have believed in something, if it's an opinion… then it's only *your* opinion. Therefore, the way you are currently looking at men and relationships, isn't the only way to look at men and relationships.

Realize that there are other opinions and ways of looking at men and relationships that are different than yours. Trust me, if what you believe about men and relationships right now isn't true, your opinions will definitely be challenged.

The Blessing & The Curse

How would you feel if you worked diligently on making me a birthday present. At its completion, it was something that you were satisfied with and personally adored? You would feel good about yourself, right? You probably would look forward to giving me my precious gift, right?

Now how would you feel, if when you brought it to me, I said, " this ain't shit", "this ain't worth anything!" How would you feel, if all I did was condemn and criticize the present you worked so hard on to give me? How would you feel if I never showed any respect and appreciation for what you created? I'll bet my ring and pinky finger that you would be heated with my ass, right?

Now imagine after I display my ungratefulness and negativity about my birthday present, I come to you and ask for another gift. Wouldn't you look at me like I was crazy? Wouldn't it appear that I had lost my damn mind? That's why, I don't understand how a woman can pray out the right side of her mouth to God, with tears in her eyes, for a man. Then say that "men ain't shit", five minutes after the "Amen".

Isn't man a creation of God? It just doesn't add up to me, babygirl. I've always thought, it was easier to give to those who appreciate and congratulate, rather than to those who cry and complain. If I really wanted something in my life, the last thing I would do is curse my blessing.

The truth is, many women wouldn't pray for a man at nine o` clock then consciously curse all men at nine fifteen. That would be crazy. However, it is something that many of you sexy ladies are guilty of. So how does it happen?

Many of you ladies don't believe that all men are good. Many of you may probably believe that there are a few good men out here. As a result, you go and beg God to make an exception. You hope God will allow you to be one of the "lucky" women to have a "good man" in their life.

The popular belief, especially within the African American community, is that "a good man is hard to find".
Contrary to public **OPINION,** I will show you that there are plenty of "good men" around. Remember, **"All men are good!"**

What do you think people do when they believe there isn't enough of something to go around? That's right, they rob, kill, and steal in order to have this limited thing. So what do you think you'll do, if you believe that there is a "good man" shortage in the world? That's right, you'll settle for anything, a married man, a man already in a relationship, anyone with a stick and two balls will do, regardless if he is a man or not. You'll allow a man to walk and talk all over you, just so that you can say you have a man (It's despicable). But how many females do you know personally, that are competing for a "good man"?

If you want to see where you are mentally, answer this question for me. How do you honestly feel, on the inside, when you find out a girlfriend has gotten married or just started a relationship with someone that she says is a "good man"? If you immediately start faultfinding and feel a little jealousy in your body, what is that really saying to you? You don't believe there are enough "good men" out here. So in your opinion, she has taken one of the few out of circulation. So instead of congratulating her on her relationship, chances are you'll start "hatin`" from the sideline. Women "hate" on other women because they don't count their blessings. There is no reason to hate on Pam for hooking with Michael. Especially when Rich is on the way (Get it). But let's get back to business.

Now let's go one step further in thought. What are you telling the Universe when you condemn for others that which you want for yourself? It sounds to me like you're cursing your own blessings.

Principle #1 - If you want a thing you must first believe you can have it and welcome it into your life affirmatively.

Stop cursing the men and blessings you want in your life. Understand, that "all men are good". There are plenty of single, available, and good brothers to go around. If you want to have a good man find you, first see the good in all men. Celebrate the good in all relationships and watch what happens.

Say It Loud

Now that we understand how important it is to affirm what we desire, I now need you to do me another favor. Let me hear you say aloud three times, with a big smile on your pretty face that **"All men are good"**. Don't just sit there reading it, go ahead and say it aloud. Let your ears hear it. **"All men are good!"**
It hurts doesn't it? I hope you understand that all of the "bullshit" and negative opinions you have about men hates to hear you say it. I know it's uncomfortable to have your comfort zone and "reality" threatened. Keep in mind that we are going some where with this. **"All men are good!"**
Isn't it scary to have your negative attitudes and erroneous beliefs about men be destroyed? All of those lies you heard mama and dem` tell you about men are being exposed. It's messed up, but mama, auntie, and all of your girlfriends that have been feeding you that "bullshit" about men have been lying to you.
Now, I don't want you calling your mother, aunts, or

girlfriends and cursing them out for doing you dirty. They did it all in love. Now don't get me wrong. Some of them were actually "playa hatin'" on you. They wanted your relationship with Romeo to end.

Some of the women that have given you advice about men, wanted you miserable, bitter, and lonely, right along side their miserable, bitter, and lonely asses. I know you might be mad and may want to square things up with them. But it's over with. What's done is done. What you can do is buy them their own copy of the book. It's at least plenty of this to go around. (Ha, ha) **"All men are good!"**

Now I need you to go one step further, stretching and expanding your comfort capacity a little bit more for me. Let me hear you say, with an even bigger smile on that lovely face, and with more confidence than before **"My father is a good man".** Say out loud **"My husband (if married) is a good man".** Say even louder **"All of the men I know are good because they have all been made in the image and likeness of a good God."**

Go ahead and say it one mo gin, repeat every last word of it. I know that it's killing you to even think of, much less say that your father is a "good man". I understand that some of you reading this book, may or may not like or associate with your father. Even if he's dead, incarcerated, or someone you've never known, say it anyway. Trust me, it is for your own benefit, *not his.*

I realize that it hurts for you to say that every man you know is "good". Especially with all of the pain, anguish, and disappointment you've experienced at the hands of some men. But don't allow Jason, Shawn, Tyrone, and Lance to have you mad with every man.

Don't think I'm crazy, but even the guy who "broke" your heart, took your virginity, and won't take care of the children you two have made, are all "good men".

It's important that you trust everything you are saying is for your well being. It's to prosper your life. Just continue to follow along.

DivaGirl - How To Have A Good Man Find You

You might find that some of this is a little too difficult to say. It may even seem like we're playing some "Psychotherapy" mind game. I just want you to know something…we are playing some "psychotherapy" mind game. But just do it anyway.

I'm respectful of your point of view and opinions about what we are doing. Just keep in mind that there are facts, experiences, and situations that are all subject to change. The truth is unchanging, and that is what you want to manifest in your world. So understand that we are slowly but surely moving away from the lies in your world. We are systematically stepping into more and more truth. Just let me drive this car babygirl. I know you might not trust men, but at least let me be the exception.

What's Really Good?

I want you to be clear. I'm not about to make statements and ask you to repeat mantras, trying to psyche you out. I'm not some Buddhist from India or down with any of this New Age mind over matter philosophy. I just want to show you a new way of looking at men and relationships.

When I ask you to say, "all men are good", it's not because I want you to sound positive and be unrealistic. I asked you to say it because it's the truth. In the introduction, I told you that nothing in this book would be any of that "Fantasy Island" crap that is flooding the market today. Please believe, I plan on keeping my word.

According to the American Heritage Concise Dictionary, "good", means being positive or desirable in nature; or high quality, suitable, appropriate. With that in mind, let's talk about something.

When most of you women use the term "good man" what are y'all usually implying? It would be safe to say, when most of you ladies are referring to someone as a "good man" it's because he is a godly/ mature/generous man, right? Absolutely **NOT**!

When most of you contemporary "new millennium"

women, say "good man", y'all are talking about someone that is tall, handsome, well built, has a good job, drives a nice car, and someone that can come into a bedroom with his forty acres and a mule.

I know some of you don't want to admit it. Just let a good looking, tall, well dressed man, getting out of a Mercedes Benz approach you; along side a unattractive (based on your standards), short, casually dressed man, that just got off the bus. Who would you give the number, that girly smile, and that "I want you look" to? Okay then, now let's move on.

Why He's Good

Man's ways and God ways are as different as night and day. Therefore, God's definitions are not man's definitions. As a result, God's "good man" and the world's "good man" are not the same man. That probably explains why in your opinion there are not enough "good men" to go around, and I believe there are enough of us out here.

You have to understand that our difference of opinion is a result of the difference of our paradigm and perspective. Now for accuracy purposes, I will use the definition of a "good man" that is found within the Bible.

To all my non-Bible readers and believers, bear with me a second. I ain't tryin' to preach my way to God, nor bore you to death with any of this. However, I have to reveal this "life-changing" truth if this book is to make any difference to your world and perception of men...iight. Now according to the Bible, God stated that "man is good" for three spiritual reasons.

Man's Three Good Reasons:

1. Man's life **Purpose** is **Good**
2. Man's **Potential** or God like nature is **Good**
3. Man's **Position** in the world is **Good**

Man's Good Purpose

> *"Then God said, "let us make man in our image, in our*
> *likeness, and let <u>them rule over</u>...all the earth."*
> (Genesis 1:26 NIV)

Principle #2 - Nothing created is without a purpose.

No man walks the earth by accident or coincidence. We are all here by specific design and for a definite purpose. Every last one of us, me, you, your father, your babyfather, your brothers, your male friends... we are all here and necessary.

Now it's a fact that many of us men walk around confused and without direction. But we are still here for a purpose. God clearly states the general reason or purpose why we are all given the opportunity of life on this earth. *"God blessed them and said to them, "Be fruitful and increase in number; fill the earth and subdue it, rule over...every living creature that moves on the ground."* (Genesis 1:28 NIV)

We have all been purposed to live like God in this World, God created. Therefore, every man you know has the same general purpose in life. We are here to live God-like in this earth. Now, how God's purpose manifest in the life of an individual is based on a person's individual gifts, passions, and decisions. I'll cover all of that at another time. I just want you to understand that underneath the confusion and ignorance so many of us men are walking around in there lies a good purpose and here's why. *If God created a good world and Man's purpose is to rule in the world. Then man's purpose is to rule in a good world. Therefore, man has a good purpose*.

Don't start trippin` just follow along. I'm going somewhere with this.

I know that it might all appear to be simple logic. But how many of us keep things simple? Just keep in mind, one of the reasons why all men are good, is because God has created man with a good purpose.

Man's Good Potential

"God **blessed them** and said to them…"
(Genesis 1:28 NIV)

The second dynamic, to "all men being good" is that, God created man with a good potential. God created your father, babyfather, and ex boyfriends, all with a good nature. I know that it's hard for you to believe but every man has a "good potential". According to the American Heritage Concise Dictionary "potential", means the capacity for growth, development, and coming into being.

When God created man he gave him the potential (nature) to look like God in the earth. If man has the potential to look like God in this earth, and it's fair to say that God is good…then man's "potential" is good. So as you can see, "all men are good!" not based on their own merits. "All men are good" by the grace and design of God.

For those of you that are still in the dark as to what I'm saying, I'll make it even simpler for you. We are all equipped with the tools to live like God. However, it's obvious that the overwhelming majority of us don't know how to use our God-like tools. Especially us men today. Understand that just because a man might not know how to use his God-like tools doesn't mean he is without them. Consequently, if you find that a man is acting like an asshole, understand that he is only proving that he doesn't know how to use his tools. Being an asshole doesn't mean a man is without "good" potential. Being an asshole doesn't mean a man isn't a creation of God.

God's definitions have nothing to do with the physical or outer dimension of life like many of us are lead to believe when we make our judgements. Man judges by appearances, God judges according to motives of the heart. Therefore, a man being "good", has nothing to do with how tall he is, how much money he has, or

34

by what he drives.

Being a "good man", according to potential is hidden from the natural eye. It's based on God's Word.

Just because you fail to **see** God's potential in all men, doesn't mean that God's potential isn't **in** all men. As a result, "all men are good" in essence. We all have a good purpose, potential, and position. To further illustrate my point think about and consider this:

When God created Adam's body, all it was…was a body. It could have been a tall, short, skinny, or a fat body. It didn't matter what it was because it was just a body. The body wasn't Adam's manhood. The body was Adam's body. Adam didn't become a living being or a good man until God breathed his breath into Adam's body.

So Adam could have possessed the face of Denzel Washington and the body of Tyson Beckford, but he was nothing but a body. Adam still wasn't a man. It wasn't until that God-like potential was given to Adam that he became a good man. Do you get it, babygirl? So without that potential, Adam would have only been a body.

"The Lord God formed the man (body) from the dust of the ground and breathed into his nostrils the breath of life (good potential) and the man became a living being (good man)" (Genesis 2:7 NIV)

BONUS (For Intellectuals Only)

Being that I really like you, I'll take you one step further. Now I have to warn you. This part may get a little technical. Just do your best to keep up, and follow along. In fact, I'll take it nice and slow.

In order for man to look like (image) God, man had to "be like", and have the nature (potential) of God. Now here is where it may get a little tricky. God's unlimited nature is spiritual and man is a spirit (so far so good). **HOWEVER**, man also lives in a limited natural body (problem).

That's why God could only satisfy his nature in man by using many bodies (human race), and with two types of earthly bodies: a **male** and a **female** physical structure. Therefore, God's potential (good nature) is equally divided into two different parts. God's potential rest in two different bodies. There is a male (good nature) and a female (good nature). We often call the two natures of God masculinity and femininity. The good nature (potential) of God dwells in both men and women in equal portions. **HOWEVER**, these two natures function differently in the world.

God's masculine energy resides predominantly in the male body. While God's feminine energy resides predominately in the female body. Remember, God's good nature (potential) is unlimited and man lives in a limited body form.

It was by God's design that his nature manifest equally but differently through man's two bodies (male and female). One of the reasons why "all men are good" is because of God's nature that dwells in the male: Not because of God's nature that dwells in female. What I'm saying is, a man is a 'good man", because he is a **man**. So don't misjudge a man as being "no good", because he isn't a **good woman**. Your father is not your mother. Your brother is not your sister. Your husband is not your wife. Your man is not your girl. **MEN are not WOMEN**! Do you understand that babygirl?

I often hear women complaining saying their "babyfather ain't shit", not because he isn't a good father. They complain, because he isn't the type of mother that she is to the child. Tyrone "ain't shit" because he doesn't act and think like a mother. See how crazy that is?

Most of the advice that women receive about men is from other women that see the world, not as men, but as women. So do you see how easy some of the common advice you receive, and comments you hear from women, regarding men can be irrational? I often hear women complaining that their man is "no good", not because he doesn't "function" as a man in the relationship. They say that he is "no good", because he isn't all of the woman that she would like for him to be. I know it sounds silly, but meditate on it for a second. Men are terrible at being women. In fact, the only men that are good at being women are "sissy's."

So if you're trying to turn a man into a woman, you're looking for a "sissy" and not a "good man". So if that's what you want then you have the problem, and not Tyrone.

Man's Good Position

The last element of God's definition of a "good man" is a man's good position. We now know that all men have a good purpose for being. We just talked about how all men have a good potential (nature) within him. Now we will discuss man's good position in the world.

When God considered the idea of man on earth, he knew there were going to be both a male and female needed to fulfill his thought. God knew a male body and nature (masculinity), as well as a female body and nature (femininity) were necessary to fulfill his will in the earth. That is why God said, *"...Let **them** rule over all the earth..."* (Genesis 1:26 NIV)

With that in mind, it's only natural that God's purpose would consist of two assignments.

*"Then the Lord God took man and put (positioned) him in the Garden of Eden to **work it** and **take care of it.**"*
(Genesis 2:15 NIV)

It's clear with that passage that God positioned man in the garden to do two things: to "work it" and "take care of it". Being that God had two assignments, two natures, and two different types of bodies (male and female). It only makes sense that God would equip each nature and body for a specific assignment.

Male was to "work" the ground. That is why Adam was positioned first. His job was development. Have you noticed how aggressive, assertive, and proactive men can be? The female was to "take care of " the ground. That's why Eve was positioned second. Her job is to "manage" whatever was developed. Have you noticed how nurturing, supportive, and accommodating you can be as a woman?

I'll get into the manifestation of our natures later on. For now I just want to reinforce that "all men are good".

According to God's definition and by his design, every man is good. That includes all of the men you currently think are "dogs", "ain't shit", and even those men that you can't stand.
"All men are good!"

Now based on God's perspective, can you see how much easier it is to say? If you continue to look at men based on your narrow and limited perspective this will continue to be a hard truth for you to accept. But whether you accept it or not, it's still true.
"All men are good!"

"Yea But, He's…"

Now I want to address your concerns, your "if, ands, or buts". I know some of you are sitting there thinking that, "all men are good", sounds good in theory. You may even appreciate the philosophy and principle behind it. But you still have your "yea but", going on inside your head.

You probably think that "all men being good" is a positive concept to believe in. But the "niggers" and "assholes" you know, ain't worth a penny with a hole in it. I feel you, I understand where you are coming from. Trust me I do.

I'm aware of the fact that some men cheat on their mates (I've been guilty of it). I'm aware of the fact that some men use and abuse the women that allow themselves to be used and abused. Believe me, I'm also conscious of the fact that some men are irresponsible and don't father their children or love their families. So trust me, I hear you loud and clearly Ms. Lady. Now you hear me loud and clearly. **"All men are good!"**

When a man cheats on his woman that doesn't mean that he is not a "good man". When a man cheats on you or on his woman, he becomes a "cheater". Just because a man is a "cheater", that doesn't mean God's design and purpose in him has changed. Therefore, he still has a good purpose, a good potential, and a good position. Now follow me.

Keep in the mind that the truth is unchanging. Now your opinion of a man may change, once he cheats. But he is still good in essence. When a man sleeps with or gets involved with another woman, those are his actions that become his experience. Now we all know that all experiences are subject to change (Thank God). As a result, that cheating man has the ability to change his actions and change his experience. I know it sounds crazy but think about it. Better yet let me ask you a question.

If a cheating man is a "bad man" or "ain't shit" in your opinion. What does that make a man who doesn't cheat? Is he a "good man"? If you said "yes" can you now see just how superficial, situational, and limited your definition of a "good man" really is? That's why your definition is an opinion and not truth. The truth is. **"All men are good!"**

Why We Do It

Man tends to think that he's defined by his actions, his possessions, and the circumstances in his life. Let me show you just how silly a thought that is to have. We are not what we do, what we have, or the circumstances we find ourselves in. No matter how positive or negative they may be that is not who we are. Now follow me.

If I make a stupid decision to rob a bank on Monday, am I stupid? Answer that for me. Am I stupid for robbing that bank? I will assume that you answered "yes". I was stupid for robbing that bank. Now was "stupid", in your definition of a good man? Of course not. So it's also safe to say that sense I'm "stupid", I'm also not a "good man", right?

Okay, now what would you say about me if on Tuesday I take all of the money from the bank robbery to cloth and feed the homeless and hungry? Am I now generous? Am I now "kind" and "loving"? Am I now a "good man"? I know it sounds funny and I don't mean to be facetious. I just want to expose the errors in our thinking. I just want to support my claim that "all men are good".

We all do different things and make some good and not so good decisions. Thank God, we're "good" not based on our appearances and actions but based on the truth of his creation.

Can you now see how limited and shallow it is to judge the quality of a man by appearances. A man's situations and circumstances isn't what qualifies him as being a good man. If you continue to judge the quality of a man by his appearance and circumstances, don't be surprised if you are still asking yourself that infamous question. "Why can't I find a good man?"

Remember baby. **"All men are good"**. Regardless if he's in prison right now or the president of the bank. **"All men are good"**. Regardless if he's tall, dark, and handsome or short, round, and looks like everything ugly, **"All men are good."**

CONCLUSION

Are you still finding it difficult to say, "All men are good"? The more you say it, the more you'll start to believe it. The more you believe that "all men are good", the more your situations and relationships with men will confirm your beliefs. Isn't that how it worked out when all you said about men was that "men are dogs", "niggas ain't shit", and "men only want one thing"?

Isn't that what you experienced when you believed in all that junk about men? Didn't your babyfather, that dude from the club, and most of the men you know confirm your belief about men?

I want you to understand, the reason why you may find it difficult to find a "good man" is not because "men are dogs". It's not because "men ain't shit". You haven't found a "good man", because your opinion of a "good man" ain't shit (Sorry but I had to go there).

DivaGirl - How To Have A Good Man Find You

A "good man", isn't limited to someone that is handsome, strong, wealthy, and successful. Although those are all positive and attractive qualities, they are only a man's circumstances and conditions. It's a truism in life that no two people are identical. It's also true that not everyone is going to be attractive or physically to your liking.

It's true that not everyone is going to possess the same amounts of money or live the same lifestyle. Some of us will be tall, some short, some rich, and some poor. It may seem unfair, but it is what it is, that's life. Therefore, it's never justifiable to measure a man by things or situations.

The "good looking" brother is no more of a man than the "unattractive" man. The "good looking" brother might receive more attention and compliments on his looks, than the "unattractive" man. But that's all it is… *more attention.* That "wealthy" man may have more luxuries and "stuff" than the brother with limited funds, but that's it.

I'm going to keep it real. That "wealthy" man might be able to buy you more things than the "poor" man can, and that may please you. Just keep in mind, it doesn't mean that the rich man can give you more *man.* **"All men are good!"**

That handsome man (the one you fantasize about), can easily lose his looks in a fire, in a freak accident, or lose them because he just lets himself go (It happens all of the time). Have you ever seen someone that you thought was fine back in the days. Then run into the same person years later and they have completely "fell off". You stand there in conversation with them, but in the back of your mind you keep saying to yourself, "what happened?"

That "rich" man (the one you lust over), can easily lose all of his money in the stock market or have his record or sports contract terminated. He can lose all of his money in a drug bust or to any of the many misfortunate occurrences people lose money to. Then all you would have is *him.*

With all of the cosmetic and surgical procedures available

today that unattractive man can become attractive, if he has a few dollars to spend. He can go buy a new face, a nice body, and a bigger penis. That unattractive man can now go purchase a "good looking man" starter kit. With the help of a surgeon, a man can go from looking like Flava Flav to Mr. Universe overnight (Well maybe I went to far with that example).

My point is for you to stop believing in all of this hype. "All men are good!" Don't measure a man unless you use the proper measuring instrument. If you wanted to know how much money was in your pockets, would you step on a scale? If you wanted to know how much you weighed, would you use a ruler? The answer to both of those questions is "no". That would be using the wrong measurement instrument.

Don't measure the quality of a man by how good or bad he looks, by how much money he has, or by any of the other temporary situations and circumstances of his life. Now don't get me wrong, you are perfectly entitled to have your preferences. If you prefer a tall, handsome, and successful man, that's your prerogative. Oh, and by the way, if that's what you're looking for, then email me ASAP. We might be able to work something out (It's a joke).

Seriously, it's important that you never think one man is "better" than the next because of what your eyes see. Your eyes can never see the whole story. If you want to measure a man's quality… **DON'T**. You don't have to measure him because..........
"All Men Are Good!"

So What Am I To Do?

$10 Million Dollar Question
■ If "all men are good", is it alright for me to date and hook up with just anyone?

$100 Million Dollar Answer
■ No! Not only "no" but **HELL NO!**

I didn't say that just because "all men are good", that every man was going to be "**right**" for you. There is a big difference between something being "**good**" and something being "**right**". Have you ever known a man and he was real cool but there was something missing? I mean the brother was nice looking, he was a good guy, but it just wasn't there. It just wasn't… "right".

Now Let Me Paint A Picture For You:

*Lets' say you and I actually meet and decide to have a candlelight dinner together over at my place. Now being the perfect gentlemen that I am (Don't believe the hype), I decide that I'm going to cook a gourmet dinner for you (I don't cook). You come over, and I have the candles burning, Luther Vandross (That's my boy) softly playing in the background, a gourmet dinner prepared for us, and to top it off, I'm looking sharper than a razor with my smell goods on. Now we have a lovely dinner. And afterwards, I bring out this homemade apple pie that I specially baked for you. The apple pie looks good, smells good, and taste like "some more" (You liking this right baby). Now let's say, I cut this pie, put some whip cream on top of it and slowly serve it too you. Sounds good huh? What would happen if you ate the pie, but unknowingly you were allergic to apples?

No matter how **good** I'm intentioned. No matter how **good** that apple pie may look. No matter how **good** that pie may taste. If you eat and allow that pie into your system, you'll have an allergic reaction. Your allergic reaction will not be the result of the pie or my intentions not being "good". Your allergic reaction will be the result of the pie not being "right" for you.

The same holds true for you with men. Although "all men are good", there are some "types" of men that you are allergic to. There are some "types" of men that are not "good" for your system.

This whole chapter has been about destroying the "good man" and "men ain't shit" paradigm within you. The truth is "all men are good!" That's the only way God has made us. Now to

*This section was written before I married my wife

continue on, with your new developing perspective on what a good man is. I need you to say out loud.

"All men are good. Every man that I know is good. However every man is not right for me." Now wasn't that easier to say and accept, than it was at the beginning of the chapter? I told you, there is a method to everything we are doing, I'm focused. Trust me, I got this babygirl.

If you continue to read along, your world as you know it will continue to change. This change isn't artificial but authentic. The change is taking place at your root. It's happening from the inside/out. So it's a change that will last. It's a beautiful thing baby, so keep on going. Don't stop reading now we have only begun. You're already one step closer to realizing that peace of mind, happiness, and having that successful relationship with not only a "good man" but with the "right man." **"All Men Are Good!"**

CHAPTER 2

LADIES FIRST

"I'm a 18-55yr old single parent of two or three kids. I work full time to support my family and to save for a rainy day. I'm a college graduate, college student, or a graduate from the school of hard knocks. I am very versatile: I'm both mother and father to my children. I have to discipline, nurture, and play with them. Plus, I have to clothe the kids and put food on the table. I hardly ever go out on dates anymore because I'm so busy with work, school, and raising my kids. Whenever I do have a minute, I go online to chat and find some male companionship. Unfortunately, the online dating thing hasn't worked out for me. I'm not one of the lucky ones that have found their 'soul mates' with the click of a mouse. I want a man but don't want to deal with the childish games they play. I don't have time for the bullshit so many men bring to the table. My days are extremely demanding because there are so many people that I have to please. There's corporate America, who says, "I'm not good enough." So I work hard to prove them wrong. There are my coworkers who are always gossiping and trying to out do me. So I have to let them know, 'I'm a grown ass woman'. There are my children, who need my attention, love, and affection. So I have to be a mommy. Then there's my church who wants me to tithe on every dollar, sow seeds, and support one financial project after another. I have to contribute financially to my church, because Pastor said that's how 'God is going to bless me'... and I want my prayers answered.. At my age, I doubt if I should feel like this. I'm tired of being alone, haven't really smiled in a while, and I'm frustrated by society's double standards and contradictions. I'm ready to just give up because I've had enough of this shit."

Today's Woman

INTRODUCTION

In the first chapter of this book my goal was to shed some light, showing that "all men are good." The next two chapters will be about exposing you to the truth, regarding who and what you are as a woman.

I must admit it may seem a little strange having a man tell you who you are as a woman. I just want you to remember that it was Adam who called Eve "woman". It was your father from whence you came. All along it has been men who have disrespected and disregarded your purpose, power, and position as a woman in the first place.

So I find it kind of ironic that here I am a young black man from the "hood" (remember we definitely ain't shit) about to expose you to the truth about your womanhood. I'm actually honored and privileged to do so.

"You are a good woman, you're beautiful, and a lady in all you do." Now you do yourself a favor and say it out loud, for the world to hear. **"I am a good woman, I'm beautiful, and a lady in all I do!"**

Now why was that easier for you to say, than it was when you first said, "All men are good" (That's dirty)?

I want us to spend the next few chapters together going back to the origins. Let's re-examine the role and nature of the woman to this whole human equation. Let's just kick back and explore the truth. Somehow, I doubt if all of that negative stuff (she can't, she won't, she's not) that they say about women is true. I believe God created a capable, necessary, and powerful woman, full of purpose. I think the only problem is, too many of you ladies are out of position. I think that many of you want to be the quarterback (throw the ball) and the receiver (catch the ball), all on the same play.

I think too many of you are overexposed and spreading yourselves too thin. As a result, you are frustrated and exhausted, thinking the game of life (your relationships, finances, career) is unfair. The truth is, you're out of position and doing things that are outside of your "success element". That's why you feel like you can't win for losing. You've been beating yourself. You have been your own worst enemy.

So let's take as much time as we need to get back on the right train and the right track. So get comfortable. If you really want to get the most out of these next two chapters, I recommend that you read them after you have taken a nice, hot, and relaxing candlelit bubble bath (I want you relaxed and fresh). This is your time in the book, where all we will talk about is you sweet lady. **"I am a good woman, I'm beautiful, and a lady in all I do!"**

All The Ladies In The House Please Stand Up

Where are all the ladies in the house? What happened to the days when it was easy to differentiate a man from a woman, a guy from a gal? Did the feminist movement kill femininity? Did rap music turn every lady into a "bitch" and "ho"? Did corporate America convert all women into competitive money chasers? These are just a few of the questions I find myself asking, as I observe today's unisex culture. This culture where men are women and women are now men.

It amazes me at just how masculine so many of you women have become. It disgusts me to witness just how feminine so many of my brothers are today. Its like females want to be men and the males want to be women, today.

Sometimes, as I'm watching one of those movies from the 50's and 60's, I marvel at the demeanor and mannerism of the men and the women of that time.

Back then, I guess it was cool to be a lady and gentlemen. To all my African American ladies, it may be a little difficult for you to look back and find a movie where you were depicted and portrayed as a lady. For some unknown reason (we know why), it has always been acceptable to show you as a whore, a nanny, a slave, or in some other degrading or servitude role. So y'all might have to search harder and use your imagination a little bit more, to locate a good time in history for you as a woman.

Back in the day, everything from the style of dress to the way people walked and spoke, displayed distinct qualities of masculinity and femininity. Men wore shoes and slacks women wore skirts and dresses. In that day, a man even spoke differently in the company of a woman than he did when he was around the fellas. Women made men prove their worthiness before he even got a date.

Today, women dress and talk just like the men. Everything from the power suits, sneakers, and Timberland boots reveal just how equal we have become. Don't get me wrong; I think it's perfectly okay for a woman to dress in any manner she prefers to cover herself in. However, I personally find nothing sexier than a woman in some stilettos, some nicely fitted pants, and a blouse. The Timberland boots and bubble winter coats on a woman just doesn't do it for me like some tight jeans and heels on a lady.

Back in the days, it took more than a Long Island Ice Tea in a club for a man to "get some" loving from a woman. Today, a man doesn't even have to open a door, bring flowers, or even show respect for a woman before she'll want to suck and hump. If a brother has a record deal or a sports contract… forget about it. That man doesn't even have to open his mouth and a woman will be ready to put him into hers.

I'm not trying to be crass. I just want you to see where I'm coming from. Today is definitely a new day in every sense of the term. Today, I see women jumping bad all in the faces of men that are much bigger and angrier than they are. I see women struggling and fighting to do and be everything that men are. Then they turn around and say they want to be treated like a lady. (Are you serious)?

This game has to stop. If something walks like a duck, quacks like a duck, and looks like a duck, then don't be mad if I treat it like a damn duck. If something walks like a man, acts like a man, and talks like a man, don't be mad if I talk to and treat it as a man. Ladies, ladies, ladies, if you want to be treated like a lady, then present a lady.

PRINCIPLE #3 - People only value what has value.

If you feel like the people around you and the men you come into contact with are disrespectful, then reassess how you've been presenting yourself. If there isn't any value about you, don't be surprised if no one appreciates what you give and offer.

I'm always amazed at how some women will blame the man for not wanting a committed relationship with them. Meanwhile, she sucked and humped him on the first date. She doesn't exercise any self-respect for herself, or show any self-confidence. Then she pressures the man into "buying" a relationship with her.

Ladies, you have to understand that men keep mental records just like you, the only thing is, we do it subconsciously. So be mindful and conscious of how you present yourself to a man. Especially, how you present yourself to a man in a high profile and influential position.

PRINCIPLE#4 - Everything has a purchase price and a maintenance price.

Would you pay three hundred thousand dollars to live in a cardboard box? Obviously not. (I sure hope you wouldn't) However, you would pay three hundred thousand dollars to live in a luxurious home of your choice.

What would you be more attentive to: a vase that cost ten dollars or a vase that cost ten thousand dollars? Exactly, you will value that which cost more. The same holds true for everyone else and every man you know. Why would he want a relationship or remain faithful and attentive to you, if there is no value there? **"I am a good woman, I'm beautiful, and a lady in all I do!"**

DivaGirl - How To Have A Good Man Find You

Wisdom gem* If you want to increase your value as a woman...
Be A Lady.

So What Is A Lady?

According to the American Heritage Concise dictionary, a "lady" is a well mannered woman and a woman who is the head of the household. I find those two definitions to be accurate for what we will discuss. I don't think I can stress the importance of mannerisms enough to you. A well mannered woman is one of life's most attractive qualities.

I remember when I was in retail I worked with a lady named Nina. Now Nina was the most "lady like", well mannered woman, I've known. She was much older than I was, but Nina had it going on something serious. If she weren't married at the time, I would've definitely put my bid in. Nina was so sexy and attractive. And it wasn't because she had the fattest butt, the prettiest face, or because she had the biggest chest in the world.

Nina wasn't even the prettiest woman in the store. It was the way Nina walked and the way she talked that was driving dudes crazy.

It was Nina's mannerism that had men mad with their girls at home. Boy oh boy, whatever happened to Nina? (Give me a second I'm reminiscing right now)?

$1 Million Dollar Question
- What does a lady act like?

$10 Million Dollar Answer
- A lady acts like God. She personifies the nurturing and feminine nature of God. She is loving, gentle, poised, and savvy.

Contrary to what the male chauvinistic patriarchal view says, a lady is gentle but not weak. She is loving but will not be walked on. She is poised but can get angry when need be. A lady is a hundred percent more than popular belief.

For years men have programmed and conditioned women to think they were inferior to men. As a result, to be ladylike meant to be timid, quiet, and a second class human. I'm here to tell you the truth and nothing but the truth Ms. Lady, you've been misguided.

A majority of what you've been led to believe about yourself as a women, was a lie. I don't care what Pastor "Know it all" told you about being a woman. I don't care what your mother was responsible for telling and showing you about being a woman. If they were wrong... *then they were wrong.*

The timid, fragile, and submissive attitude that is perceived to be ladylike, is not what a lady is... **THAT'S A SLAVE.** A lady is not what this male dominated society has taught you.

Women are equal to but different from men. It's no accident that the male and female anatomy is designed differently. It's also not a coincidence that men and women have different emotional and mental tendencies.

We are supposed to be different as men and women but equal as humans.

Wisdom gem* It's possible for things to exist as different but still be equal

Example: 4+4=8 and 6+2=8

Those are two different set of integers that when added equals the same whole.

BOTTOM LINE...

Ladies you don't have to act like a man in order to be equal to men.

Soil Of The Earth

Why do men and women struggle so much with the fact that we are different? Men and women are the only creatures, to my knowledge, who battle with their identities and role in society. I've never seen a male cat struggle with his maleness or a female tiger struggle with her femaleness. The sun doesn't try to be the moon nor does the moon try to be the sun. Yet, everyday we have men who think they are women and vice versa.

When God created Adam and Eve, he didn't want Eve to be like and function as Adam, nor did he want Adam to be like and function as Eve. What God wanted was for Eve to be Eve and function like God, and he wanted Adam to be Adam and function like God.

So if God didn't want his man being a woman, or his woman being a man in the beginning, then what makes you think he wants it now? When God formed Adam, he formed him from the ground then put him in the Garden to "work".

With Eve, her process was different. God formed Eve from the rib of Adam and the first thing God gave her was a "relationship". They were both given something to do. Adam had to "work" the ground and Eve had to "nurture" it. As a result, Adam was given a "*position*" and Eve a "*relationship*".

Ladies, ladies, ladies, it's God's will and by his design that you are "nurturing" and "relational". Nurturing meaning, it's natural for you to want to raise your children. It's in your nature, for you to want to see the relationship with your man grow and improve. It's natural for women to talk about their kids and significant others, before their jobs and positions.

Women are here to make our relationships work. Women are the "heart" and "soil" of the earth. Men are the "head" and "gardeners".

Let's take a look at the reproductive process as an example of our natural functions.

In order for a man and woman to reproduce physically and make a baby, certain truths must exist. Now be clear, I am not a doctor nor will I attempt to be. So I'm going to keep it real basic and simple.

The Five Truths of Reproduction
    1. A man must release (plant) a seed (sperm cell)
    2. A woman must receive the seed (soil)
    3. The seed (sperm cell) must be planted into fertile soil
    4. Woman must nurture the development of the seed to harvest
    5. Woman must release the fruit of the seed at harvest time

    I realize that I'm getting technical again, but follow me anyhow. As a woman, you have been created to nurture and nurse the developmental process of humanity, physically as well as mentally and emotionally. There is something that a woman possesses which causes things to grow and flourish. It's called the *"woman's touch"*.

    Women are the "soil of the earth". It's critical to all of humanity that women remain fertile and good ground. When I say "fertile", I'm not only implying physically but also mentally and emotionally.

    We need the woman back in her natural position making this world feel warm and loving again. It's like now that so many women have stopped loving and nurturing we are all suffering from this cold harsh world.

    Ladies, you need to understand that there are four seasons in a year. There are different seasons in your life. However, in the midst of a cold winter or hot summer you can remain fertile. Just because the last relationship didn't work out, you can remain optimistic about this one or the next.

    Just because Tyrone hurt you, it doesn't mean you have to shut down emotionally and become cold, cutting off your sensitivity and femininity. Just because Sean wasn't deserving of your love and faithfulness doesn't mean you have to take out your pain on your children.

    Life will challenge you and send you through some changes. People will disagree with you, disappoint you, and work to deplete you of your vigor.

However, you remain fertile, you remain loving, gentle, nurturing, and sweet. You are a lady the "soil of the earth". If you go bad, we will all rot and wither away.

"I am a good woman, I'm beautiful, a lady in all I do!"

The Myth Of The "Good Woman"

Why do so many women assume that a "good woman" is someone that is strong and independent? I don't know how many women I have met that told me they were a "good woman", because they were "strong and independent." The funny thing is, they say it with an attitude. Then they roll their head like they're doing the snake on me (What's that all about).

Being strong and independent is all good. They are positive qualities to have, but they can become a problem in a relationship with a man. Strength is relative and no one is truly independent in this life (We all receive help).

If you can lift 200lbs of weight, would you consider yourself strong? Now what if I can lift 250lbs of weight. Am I stronger than you? In this case, I can say that I'm stronger because I can lift more weight than you can.

Now what would you think and say, if I'm six foot seven inches tall and weigh two hundred and eighty pounds. (I'm actually only 6'2) Meanwhile, you are a petite five foot three inches tall and weigh one hundred and ten pounds soaking wet. Am I still stronger than you?

I want you to see just how many different variables go into making an accurate judgement. In order to fairly compare two things, you need apples to apples and oranges to oranges.

Women are often measuring their strength in relation to a man. Some women say that they are strong because they can curse, win an argument, or dominate and control weak minded individuals. If a woman can dominate a man, she might think she is the strongest woman in the world (my opinion)

The strength of a man and the strength of a woman, are two

completely different strengths. A man's strength is power. A woman's strength is beauty. Now I can hear all of my feminist and bodybuilding ladies losing their cool right now because of what I just said.

So here, I'll say it again. A man's strength is **POWER**. A woman's strength is **BEAUTY**. Have you ever wondered why it's so easy for a beautiful woman to make a powerful man weak? (Read the story of Samson and Delilah, Judges chapter 16)

Think about it. Isn't it attractive for you ladies to hear a man with a strong and powerful voice speak? Now think about if a woman sounded and looked like Barry White. (May he rest in peace)

My male friends and I, are often joking about how powerful women are. Sadly, many of you women are so busy trying to out do men that y'all don't even know where your strength lies. There is something about a pretty woman that carries herself like a lady. It makes even the strongest man weak in the knees. (I can testify to that personally)

When a woman says that she is strong, it shouldn't be due to the fact that she's aggressive, confrontational, stubborn, or hard. The strength of a woman is her virtue, femininity, and her presence. The things that make a man strong are not the things that make a woman strong, and vice versa. What man finds a woman with huge muscles attractive? What man is attracted to a vulgar, loud mouth, and disrespectful woman?

Having big muscles are cool, if you're a body builder. Being loud and vulgar works well if you're a comedian. However, on an average day to day basis, those characteristics are not a good look for a lady. Trust my call on that one.

Ladies, ladies, my sexy ladies, being a *man* doesn't work for you as a *woman*. Therefore, don't measure your strength like a man would measure his strength. Be strong as a woman. Be strong as a lady. Do your own thing.

Independent Women

I'm personally tired of hearing women say, "I'm independent, I do for myself, I pay my own bills." *NEWS FLASH*…you should pay own bills…they're ***your bills*** , babygirl. That's not being "independent" that's called being **"responsible."** So what, you're special now because you pay your own rent, cell phone bill, and car note? Come on baby, expect more of yourself and get more from yourself. Like I mentioned earlier, no one is truly independent. We all receive and need assistance to get anywhere in life. You are where you are right now because someone has helped you along the way.

Independence (whatever that is) can easily become selfishness or stubbornness when one goes too far with it. It's perfectly fine and beneficial for you to handle your business. It's natural to take care of the things you are capable of taking care of. On the other hand, it's counterproductive to think that you can handle everything. It works against you to think you are "*superwoman*".

PRINCIPLE #5 - People need people, men need women, women need men, kids need parents, and parents need kids.

Would you interview for a company that made it clear they weren't hiring? Would you help someone that said they didn't need your help? The chances of you doing so are slim to none. The same holds true, if as a women, you walk around with this "I'm strong and independent" sign on your chest.

People will overlook your cries and pour more and more of life on your shoulders, with no regard to the toll it may take on you. People only see what you show them. So if you're showing people "*superwom*an", don't get mad when you have to be everything to everybody. People will expect you to do all there is to do out in this demanding world.

Don't misconstrue what I'm saying, being strong as a

woman and responsible is a glorious thing. Being as strong as a man and independent is a turn off to men. Now remember, I said I was gonna be honest with you. No man wants a woman that doesn't have a need for him. The world won't help the woman that can "do everything". That's why "*superwoman*" dies early.

It's in a man's nature to look for and measure himself, based on a position of power. Consequently, having a job, money in his pocket, or some symbolic possessions of success is important to his esteem. So with that in mind, what type of message and vibe are you creating when you come off or flat out say, "I'm strong and independent" to a man that needs to be needed?

Your intentions may be right, but the message is all wrong. A man wants and needs to be needed. Let me say that again just in case you missed it. *A man wants and needs to be needed.* Understand that I didn't say "*burdened*" or "*nagged*" but **needed.**

$1 Million Dollar Question
■ So what are you saying Rich? Am I to act like a bimbo or like some woman that doesn't have a clue?
$10 Million Dollar Answer
■ Absolutely not!

I would recommend that you do the same thing every prestigious company does when it's hiring. You first make it known that you're hiring (There's a need). You then interview several candidates (Date). On your interviews, make it clear to each candidate that your company has standards and only hires the best and "right" person for the job. When you find someone that is "right" (not only good) for the job, hire him. Give the dude all of the benefits and rewards of being with your company.

In laymen terms, all you have to do sweetheart is be yourself. Show that there is space in your life for a man. Let brothers know that since you have so much to give (value) he has to come to the table correct, complimenting you.

DivaGirl - How To Have A Good Man Find You

Be clear, you don't have to walk around arrogantly or with a no nonsense attitude. Have fun and be positive. (Be fertile) You'll meet the "right" man sooner than you think.

Keep in mind that "strong and independent" mentality is counterproductive in this demanding world. It also doesn't work well in relationships. Be beautiful, be virtuous, be noble, be feminine, be that special lady that you are, the world needs that. Leave the "strong and independent" thing for all the overworked and stressed out women that "can't find a good man". Let me hear it sweetheart.

"I am a good woman, I'm beautiful, and a lady in all I do!"

Forget What "They" Say!

Society works hard to make you feel unattractive, overweight, and undesirable. Most women feel that if they don't have the "video girl" or "stripper" look going on that they don't have it going on. That's just some more of the bullshit you eat and let contaminate your system.

Babygirl, you are beautiful whether slim, short, tall, heavy set, petite, black, white, brown, or yellow. If there is one thing that I want you to take from this book, let it be that you come to accept yourself and all of yourself as good and beautiful. Jennifer Lopez, Beyonce, Halle Berry, Lisaraye and all the other women that you see grazing the covers of magazines are all beautiful women. So please don't get me wrong.

However, Oprah Winfrey, Monique, Ricki Lake, and all of the other women that don't make it to the cover of a magazine (unless they own it) are beautiful as well.

Don't you ever let a man's preference make you feel unattractive or undesirable. It's a fact that here in America we've been programmed to worship "White America". I mean we have been conditioned to make our judgments based on "white" standards.

In America today, it's a fact that the overwhelming majority

58

of them that make the laws, head our major social institutions, and they that control much of what we see and hear are white older males. Therefore, it's critical that you are conscious of what is being communicated to you when you watch television, when you listen to popular music, and when you read the many women's magazines that flood the market.

If "they" are telling you that you're not pretty enough or slim enough beware. If "they" are telling you that your chest is too small, that your butt is too big, pay attention. If "they" are telling you that you're too dark, that you're too light, that your hair is too short, watch your pocket book.

Let me just tell you a little secret about "they". "They" ain't Sugar Honey Ice Tea. "They" are liars and manipulative business people that slave for money. If they can convince you that you're overweight... then they can also sell you some "miracle" diet pills. Those pills that are suppose to make you lose thirty pounds in three days.

Now if you believe that there are some pills out there that will make you lose thirty pounds in three days, then I have a bridge that I want to sell you babygirl. (For real)

You have to understand that this culture and business climate exploits and then capitalizes on people's weaknesses and insecurities. So understand that "they" want you feeling unattractive, because "they" have some cream, some pills, or some program to sell you.

Wisdom Gem* If you want to rid yourself of your insecurities then accept yourself as you are and not as you want to be and don't compare yourself to anyone else.

Understand, that I don't think there is anything wrong with wanting to lose weight, with wearing a weave, or altering your look in any way. I just don't want you thinking that unless you do those things, you'll remain unattractive or undesirable. You are fine just as you are.

However, health, exercise, and grooming yourself are all positive for ones well being and esteem. I think it's beneficial that you watch your weight, exercise, and keep your hair, feet, and nails done. It's all a part of being a woman.

Just remember, Beyonce, J Lo, Oprah, and Star Jones are all beautiful women. Your beauty isn't predicated on what "they" say. Your beauty is greater than how you look. Your beauty is who you are. That you must know.

"I am a good woman, I'm beautiful, and a lady in all I do"

CONCLUSION

I hope that I have inspired a new attitude and enhanced your sense of self in this chapter. Babygirl, it's cool and attractive to be feminine, ladylike, virtuous, and noble. There may be those who misjudge you as being "stuck up". Some may even call you "booshi", but it's all good.

Whenever something is expensive those who can't afford it "hate" on it. So if that happens, realize that your value has gone up. By returning to or enhancing the lady in you, you will vibrate at a greater frequency and attract better qualities into your life. If you want to deal with a gentlemen be a "lady", not a snob. If you want influence with others be a "lady", not a bitch.

Femininity is the power of God at work in his female creation. Fearful and ignorant men have worked hard to keep women down for ages. The history books are written, the Holy Scriptures are interpreted, and art portrayed to make you women feel second class.

The good news is that today is a new day. Women are realizing many "successes" in areas they struggled for equality and recognition within for centuries. There are women CEO's, lawyers, doctors, athletes, and even women soldiers today. I applaud you all on your many victories and accomplishments. I do however have a concern.

My concern is that so many women have focused on and

fought so hard to be equal with men that many have become men in nature (masculine). Remember men and women are equal but different. I say **EQUAL** but **DIFFERENT**.

If you want to do the things that men do, don't do them with the strength and power of a man. Do them with the beauty and elegance of a lady. The world needs you to put the "midas" touch on things. Being a lady is a privilege that God only gave to his female creation.

So contrary to what RuPual may lead you to believe, being lady like is for the women only. Don't you ever let a man convince you that you're second class, unworthy, or incapable because you are a woman. Don't think being sensitive, soft, and gentle, are signs of weakness. Walk tall, be graceful, and show the world that God is also nurturing, feminine, and beautiful. Be a lady first!

CHAPTER 3

"YOU GO GIRL: THE
MULTIFACTED WOMAN

"She gets up while it is still dark; she provides food for her family and portions for her servant girls. She considers a field and buys it; out of her earnings she plants a vineyard."
(Proverbs 31:15-16 NIV)

INTRODUCTION

The last chapter we talked about the nature and beauty of being a woman, of being a lady. Now let's talk about that which you are capable of as a woman. Let's talk about your potential. The greatest lie the devil ever told through man was that you're not capable, you can't achieve, and that you don't deserve to be happy, fulfilled, and prosperous in life... *because you are a woman.* It's your God given right and responsibility to be happy, satisfied, and successful in the life you choose to live.

In this country African American and Hispanic people are suggestively led to believe many negative and limited things about themselves. Yet, no one segment of people has been more negatively conditioned to think of themselves as inadequate, than women have.

62

DivaGirl - How To Have A Good Man Find You

Now I want you to put two and two together. What is the Black and Hispanic woman led to believe about herself in America? Keep in mind many of the men she is to build with are dead, incarcerated, hopeless, or chasing "waterfalls".

Is it any wonder that she doesn't believe in the "American Dream" any more? Is it easy for her to believe in marriage when it appears that all men want to be are players, pimps, and Don Juans? How can she believe in starting that business, when she has to raise the kids all by herself and has no time? Why would she believe that she can buy that home, when she's underpaid and in debt up the roof? Is it easy for her to believe that we live in a country where there is enough wealth for everyone, when she can barely manage to pay her bills at the end of the month?

I refuse to sit up here and ignore the everyday "struggle's" and "battles" that all woman face. Especially the struggles of my Black and Hispanic women. (I love my White and Asian ladies as well)

I remember when it was common among African American people to believe that they had to be twice as good and work twice as hard as their White counterparts to succeed. Yet in spite of all of that no one had to work harder than the woman.

So what is a woman to do when the "game" is set up for her to be a fan and spectator, meanwhile "she's got game"? How is she to feel about herself when men keep trying to push her to the sidelines to be an observer?

Why can't she preach and head a ten thousand member congregation on Sunday? Why can't she become President of the United States, or perform the unthinkable?

In this country, we compete, compare, and condemn everything that is not like us (It's the American way). So is it any surprise that certain power structures vehemently strive to keep women excluded from the "dream".

I'll tell you a little secret. It's hard for a man to compete and lose to a woman. It's difficult for a man to compare himself to a woman (Unless he has some sugar in his tank). Remember, you need apples to apples. Trust me, men operate on too much ego for it to go down like that.

Men have been condemning women for ages, because you all are different from us physically, emotionally, and mentally.

That's why, I'm so impressed by all of you ladies who persevere and produce in spite of. I tip my hat to all of the women college graduates, single mothers, and female executives that are holding it down for all women across the globe.

I salute all of the female entrepreneurs, teachers, and professionals, making power moves in this world. I also tip my hat to the blue-collar women that get their nails dirty during the day, but who are ladies at night. "You go girl!"

A woman has to extend and sacrifice a lot to be a good mother, a loving friend, a loyal employee, a good lover, a successful businesswoman, and a noble wife. So to do so shows a lot of character. "You go girl!"

This chapter is a celebration for some and a challenge to others. The objective is to help you tap into your potential and to walk in the purpose of your heart. What's the point of having a "good man", when you aren't satisfied with yourself as a woman? All you gonna do is ruin the relationship and strengthen any negative beliefs you have about yourself, men, and relationships. Self-sabotage is a common demon many women live with.

Many women psyche themselves out of their own happiness and success by creating many self imposed obstacles. The good thing is if it's a self imposed belief that is your Goliath right now, you can overcome it just like David did. You can overcome that voice that tells you, "you're not smart enough, you're too young", or that "you're too old". You can overcome that voice that tells you "you're not pretty enough", "you don't have enough money to start", or that voice that says, "you're a woman and women can't do that".

Let me be the first to tell you babygirl. You are smart enough, your age doesn't matter, you're beautiful, be the first woman to do it, you can achieve it, you can have it. "You go girl!"

Mommy, Mommy, Mommy

This is for all of the sexy ladies out there with children. This is for all of my baby's mommas, momma's, babies mommas, momma's, mommas. **"You are more than just a mother!"**

I realize that when God blessed you with a child, your world as you knew it changed immediately. I don't have the make up to understand the power and transformation of motherhood. Therefore, I won't arrogantly sit up here and pretend that I do.

I appreciate the fact that you have embraced motherhood and wear the title with such honor (I wish more fathers did it). It's beautiful to see you raise and nurse your offspring so lovingly. There isn't a greater force in the world than a woman's love for her child. You all will swim across any ocean, climb any mountain, and walk into a life threatening situation for your children (I know my mother would).

What would this world be like if all of the loving mothers left the earth? What would happen if mommy, ma, big momma, and grandma were gone? It's clear that without mothers we are dead. Amazingly we have somehow managed to get by without fathers??? But we are doomed without mothers.

Your role as a mother is an honor. It's a noble title that God had bestowed on you as a woman. Never ever regret becoming a mother. Even if the timing was bad, the baby's father was "wrong", or if you had to temporarily put school, your career, or your dreams on hold. Never regret becoming a mother.

I understand that for many of you the role of mommy can be overwhelming at times. Especially, when you have to be mommy and daddy for more than one child.

I understand that for many of you single mothers, with two or more kids, it may be difficult for you to relax, think a new thought, or to plan a course of action to go back to school, improve your career, or to realize that childhood dream. I'm here to tell you that **"You are more than just a mother!"**

DivaGirl - How To Have A Good Man Find You

You are smart, talented, gifted, sexy, funny, and valuable, even if all of those qualities are buried underneath frustration, confusion, and stress. For all of you stay at home moms, you are still talented, gifted, and full of purpose. Just because you're a mommy, doesn't mean you are disabled, unnecessary, or invaluable? Just because you have two or more kids to raise, doesn't mean your dreams as a kid must die.

Having two or more babies fathers, doesn't mean you're a "ho", promiscuous, or that you have to act desperate and lower your standards as a lady, in order to be with a man. You will find a good man. Better yet a good man will find you. He will love you and your kids (Trust me on that).

Just because you've been out of the job market for years, doesn't mean you cannot sharpen up and develop new skills. Being a mother doesn't disqualify you from becoming a graduate, a professional, or an entrepreneur. Being a mother doesn't stop you from becoming a model, actress, singer, or entertainer. Being a mother only makes you a... *mother.*

As a mother you don't have to stay in an abusive or unhealthy relationship for the kids or financial security sake. Trust me, I do understand and know personally what it feels like to have to do what you have to do. I know what it's like to have your back against the wall. If you're currently trapped in an unhappy situation, know that all things are for a season or reason. You will turn things around babygirl. Believe in yourself and know that God is on your side. **"You are more than just a mother!"**

Yea "But", "I Should", "I Can't"

There you go again showing off that big ole "but" of yours. No matter how lovely that "but" is, I'm really not trying to see your "but" right now (Maybe later on). Your "but" is too heavy of a load for you to carry. Maybe you do need a "but" reduction? Maybe your but is too big? (I'm laughing hard right now) Seriously, words are the life force of creativity and manifestation.

Your words are what shapes your thoughts, attitudes, and feelings. If you say false and negative things out of your mouth, don't be surprised if you are always in the middle of some drama or negative situation.

PRINCIPLE# 6- Negativity loves and breeds negativity.

If your conversation about yourself, men, and life is negative, expect to see the world as half empty. If you always have something negative to say, expect to be depressed and to feel run down. Negativity loves and breeds negativity. That's the way it is and that's the way it will be.

In my study and deep introspection, I have found three words that destroy, hinder, and sabotage any effort with the quickness. The words "can't", "should", and "but", are all curse words. I'm quite sure that you've thought "ass", "bitch", and "fuck" where all curse words, but they're not. Those words can be interpreted as being vulgar and inappropriate, but they are not curse words.

The sooner you can eliminate "can't", "should", and "but" from your conversation, the more blessed you will be. Let me illustrate what I'm talking about. Now listen to the difference in each of these statements.

STATEMENT A:
"Baby I'm in love with you. I want for us to get married, **BUT** I think I **SHOULD** be at least forty years old before I take that step. So we **CAN'T** get married for another fourteen years.

STATEMENT B:
"Baby I'm in love with you so much. Will you marry me?"

Which one of those statements would you want to hear from that special man, statement A or statement B? Obviously you chose statement B.

Did you notice how confusing and powerless statement A was? "Should", "can't", and "but", kills, steals, and destroys. Notice how clear, certain, and confident statement B sounds. There isn't anything to negate, diminish, or complicate the message. Now think about how often you use those three words.

"I **should** be married by now." "I want to go back to school **but** my kids needs me." "I **can't** pay off all of this debt." Just listen to yourself and the words you use to describe your situations. Now do you understand why you feel so confused and depressed? You've been cursing yourself and sabotaging your peace of mind, happiness, and success for too long.

It's sad to admit it, but you've been kicking your own ass. Eliminate the "should", "can't", and "but" from your conversation, and watch your confidence, concentration level, and clarity of purpose increase. Babygirl, it's all up to you. Your life is in your own hands. If you want it, you can have it. It's yours for the taking. There is no "should", "can't", or "but" about it. You're more than you think.

Wisdom gem* If you want to eliminate the "should", "can't", and "but" curse from your life and increase your blessings then do this. For every time you catch yourself "cursing" yourself, "bless" yourself. What I mean, is for every time you say, "I should", "I can't", or "yea but", put a quarter in your piggy bank, run an extra minute on the treadmill, drink another glass of water. Just do something that will enhance your life.

It doesn't matter if you're a young single mother of one or an older married woman with two or more kids. **"You are more than just a mother!"**

Understand sweetheart that before the kids, you had a life that you were living. Being a mother now doesn't make you one dimensional. The sky is the limit for you. There is still much more besides raising your kids to be quality people that you can achieve. The doors are still open and the world still awaits you. God still wants to use you. We all need your purpose fulfilled and potential realized.

The Professional

This is for all of my working class, getting money for themselves, and "power" title holding ladies. As much as you may enjoy the title they gave you. As much as you love to do what you do for a living. I understand that you've sacrifice much, fought hard, and overcame many obstacles to get where you are right now. However, I have some news for you. **"You are more than your job title!"**

I realize that you take pride in the contributions you make in corporate America as a professional. We all benefit from you being a positive and productive force in the world. However, **"You are more than your job title"**. You are capable of more than your job description details.

Now, I want to address an issue that I see growing between the professional woman and the every day Joe Blow. Just because you have a degree Ms. Lady, doesn't make you smarter or a better person than anyone, especially the man in your life.

PRINCIPLE # 7 – Everyone is knowledgeable of some things and ignorant of much more.

Being a college graduate, a college student, and a professional in the market place is all good. However, it doesn't make you better than anyone that may not possess your academic or professional achievements.

I only bring this up because many of you professional women need to be humbled. Many of you all need to be broken down before you are empowered anymore. I'm really not trying to be too hard on you professional ladies. I just want to make sure you get off of that high horse and walk with both feet on the ground.

I'm proud of your accomplishments babygirl. Don't let my realness turn you off. For me, there is nothing more attractive than an accomplished and humble woman.

Understand, that you are more than your accomplishments. It's so important that you grasp that truth and digest it thoroughly. You are who you are with or without that title. You are capable of much more with or without that particular career you have chosen. There is more to you than you are currently expressing. There is more to life than your job and career. You're greater than a title.

Babygirl, don't forget to take time to "play" and to enjoy life. If you're fortunate enough to conceive a child, embrace the blessings of motherhood with open arms (You can handle it). Don't work too hard that you don't have any energy to hang out, to make love, or to enjoy the sun, moon, and stars. Don't allow yourself to be boxed in. Don't allow yourself to become one dimensional.

It's okay for you to have that baby, to switch careers, and to go out with that brother from the mailroom. It's okay for you to take a day off and just pray, play, and pleasure yourself. Open up to the other dimensions of yourself. It's okay to add more blessings into your life.

"You are more than your job title. You are capable of more than you are currently doing. You can have more prosperity in your life."

Open Up There's More

My theme so far has been "you're more". Open up your heart, open up your mind, and let yourself dream again. Take the time to discover what you really want out of life. The fact that you've picked up this book indicates that having a "good" man and satisfying relationship with him is important. However that's just one dimension of your life.

How do you really want to earn a living and contribute to the world? What do you want to instill in your children? How will the world know that you were here? Do you want to travel, write a book, record a CD, or discover the cure for AIDS (the real cure)? There are no limits on you.

Open yourself up to the world of possibility that exist. Don't be surprised that we are talking about more than just having a good man find you. It's about you becoming more and all that you can be **first**. You can have a "good" man and create a bad situation just because you aren't happy and content with yourself.

Your womanhood is essential to your well being and overall expression of life. That's why I would recommend that you get a blank sheet of paper and reexamine what your values are, what your goals are, and what your priorities are in life.

PRINCIPLE #8 - In order for a thing to enter in, there must be an opening for it to come through.

If you want more out of life, open up and receive it. It's possible for you to have good relationship, a satisfying career, and a blessed family. It's more than possible for you to have money to enjoy, peace of mind, happiness, and success. Just open up to the possibility first.

Open up and let that "good" man into your world (He won't hurt you). Open up and let your children grow up (They will be okay). Open up your world, you are worthy and capable of so much more. You are an awesome woman. You are multifaceted and can achieve big dreams. "You go girl!"

CONCLUSION

Are you now convinced that you got it going on (ebonics)? There are so many dimensions and levels that you have probably ignored. There's your spirit woman, she needs to be fed constantly with prayer, truth, and meaning.

There's your emotional capacity, it needs affection, appreciation, and agreement. There's your mental dimension, it needs to be stimulated with ambition, positive energy, and challenge. There's your physical, it needs nutrition, pleasure, and exercise. I could go on and on about just how multifaceted and multidimensional you are. It's important that you satisfy your many needs.

You're more than a mother and a department manager. You're more than your bank account and the debt you owe. You're more than a high school dropout or church member. Babygirl, you are so much more than meets the eye. The reason why this is so important is because it will keep you from selling yourself short.

You don't want to sabotage your peace of mind, happiness, and success. The fact that you've picked up this book shows that you are looking for the answers. You want more and deserve to have it. Understand that you can have it and will have it. Now open up and let it happen.

Ask for a promotion; give that brother who's been knocking your door down some rhythm. Go back to school, attend some seminars, read more books. Pray more, read the Bible, fast for a day. Create a financial plan, save some money, start investing in yourself. Take a day off, take a vacation, put the kids to bed early, ask someone if they will baby sit (mama and dem` they owe you for lying). Go out dancing, write that book, romance yourself, and tell the truth about your needs. Inspire your man to step up, rock his world. Set a positive example for the younger women that are watching you. Carry yourself as a lady, be happy, be extraordinary, and be successful. "You go girl!"

CHAPTER 4

BITCHES AND HO'S: DADDY'S LITTLE GIRL AIN'T LITTLE NO MO...

"Like a gold ring in a pigs snout is a beautiful woman who shows no discretion." (Proverbs 11:22 NIV)

"Bitches ain't shit but ho's and tricks"
Snoop Dogg

INTRODUCTION

The last two chapters, I was sweet, gentle, and nice (A lover). I was a coach, a motivator, a positive breath and influence. This chapter will definitely be different. From the outset I vowed to be faithful and true to you, therefore I have to give it to you rough and tough as well.

This chapter will be more aggressive and forceful. I'm coming strong with this one. Reader Discretion Strongly Advised.

As much as I love you women and appreciate God for all that he has put in you all. I still have a bone to pick. There are some bad apples and weeds among you. There are two women in particular that are a disgrace to womanhood. These two women make it hard for the rest of y'all to get along peacefully.

These two women are everywhere you turn. They are in every nightclub in the world, on the street corners. They are strong on every college campus. These two women are in corporate America with the sophisticated titles and powerful positions. They are destroying the community and unfortunately these women are holding it down in a big way in the church.

If you are wondering whom the culprits are that I am talking about, they are Ms. Bitch and Ms. Ho (Not Ms. Ho from the nail salon).

The most disturbing thing about Ms. Bitch and Ms. Ho is that they have a strong influence on so many females today. Would you believe they have other females aspiring to be "bitches" and "ho's"? I know it's bananas right? It just goes to show what time it really is out here.

I know Eleanor Roosevelt, Harriet Tubman, Princess Diana, and all the other great women that have graced this earth, are disgusted because of this. Ms. Bitch and Ms. Ho are giving women a bad look, any way you dice it.

Being the man that I am, I plan on doing every lady reading this book a favor. I'm about to put Ms. Ho and Ms. Bitch on blast. I'm blowing their cover, for us all to see. It's time that a man and not only the self righteous, feminist, and Nubian sisters go at these women.

Please be warned that if at this point you just happen to be Ms. Bitch or Ms. Ho, I'm about to offend the "bitch" and "ho" in you.

Daddy's Little Girl

Fatherlessness is an epidemic in this country, especially within the African American community. Men are running away from the opportunity of fatherhood like it's a deadly disease. It's a fact that the number of female headed households is increasing in this country, right along side the cost of living.

It's a fact that many are growing up without a "healthy" sense of what a father really is. Contrary to many opinions, a father is more than the dude who sexed your mother, got her pregnant, and then dropped her off in the middle of nowhere. A father is more than that dude you look like but never see.

Your father is why you are here to begin with. I know we've all been taught to worship mommy and to tolerate daddy. But daddy is the cause.

PRINCIPLE #9 - You came *from* you father and *through* your mother.

Listen and meditate on that for a moment. If this is true, and it is, then daddy's role is greater than many of us would like to believe.

Daddy isn't only crucial to the male child like it has been well documented and often studied. We are coming to see just how important daddy is in the male child's development into manhood. Unfortunately, we don't study with the same intensity and zeal the affects of daddy on the female child. If daddy is the cause of us being here, then that also includes the female child. If daddy's role is critical to the male child's development into manhood, then daddy's role must also be critical to the female child's development into womanhood.

How a little girl interacts with her father and the nature of that relationship, is extremely influential to the woman she becomes later on in life. Daddy's little girl grows up fast and becomes another man's girlfriend, fiancée, and a wife some day. Daddy's little girl becomes a little boy's mother one day. Daddy's little girl definitely grows up and matures. But grows and matures into what?"

It's a fact, that daddy is a little girl's first male encounter. The love, attention, and affection a little girl receives from her father, sets the stage for the love, attention, and affection she'll crave from other males later on. Remember, daddy is purposed to be the first male not the only male in a woman's life.

Daddy's presence, his touch, his voice, his exchange with his little girl, is pivotal to her emotional development as a woman.

DivaGirl - How To Have A Good Man Find You

It's my personal belief (opinion), that as a female you can learn how to be a woman spiritually from the Word and Spirit of God. You can learn how to be a woman mentally and physically from another woman (mother, aunts, sisters, etc). However, it's my personal belief that a female learns how to be a woman, emotionally from a man (father, boyfriend, etc).

Womanhood is the feminine manifestation of God's presence, power, and purpose into the world through his female creation. Therefore, emotional development is essential to womanhood. Being that daddy is the first male, he is the foundation to a woman's emotional development.

With fatherlessness crippling so many families and communities, many women today are emotionally underdeveloped. When I say "underdeveloped", I mean that many women are still craving the fundamental emotional impact of daddy. They want to be loved, given the attention from, and receive the affection from daddy's voice, hands, lips, and arms. Many women are craving daddy's purpose in their lives.

For many little girls, daddy was absent and daddy was abusive. For others, daddy was loving; he was a positive force in their world. Daddy was their hero.

In a perfect world, every little girl would be daddy's little girl and grow up emotionally healthy. If that were to happen, so many women wouldn't suffer the emotional pain and emptiness they feel when they look to a boyfriend for daddy's satisfaction. By nature, women function more according to their emotions than men. Remember, women are to "take care" of the earth.

Women are "nurturing". Therefore, emotions play a huge role in a woman's life. I believe that Ms. Bitch and Ms. Ho are extremely underdeveloped emotionally. It's mainly because daddy didn't do his job.

So daddy's little girl has grown up to become Ms. Bitch and Ms. Ho. Damn, damn, damn ...daddy's little girl ain't little no mo.

Bitches & Ho's

What is it that makes a woman a "bitch"? What is it that makes a woman a "ho"? I'm from the school of thought that nothing is either bad or good in and of itself. I believe it's the use of, or interpretation of a thing that makes it either good or bad. I know that the average person would say that to be a "bitch" or a "ho" is a bad thing. However, there are those individuals that view being a bitch or a ho, as a cool thing (Would you believe that). To remain fair, we will look at both the negative side to begin a "bitch" or "ho" as well as the "cool" side.

Negative side

I remember one night, my business partner and myself were up to about six in the morning discussing what it is that makes a woman a "ho". After much analyzing and reflecting, we ended up with something that is close to the opening quote in this chapter. A "ho" is a woman that shows no sexual discretion or exercise any control over what she does sexually.

A "ho" is basically a woman that does any and every thing sexually with any and everybody. Now everyone has a right to have their own interpretation and definition of what a "ho" may be. I think it's safe to say that someone's negative definition of a "ho", will be close to the one we will use.

A "ho" is that female who sleeps with her "boyfriend", two of his friends, and that smooth brother who bought her a drink in the club. A "ho" is a female that almost every dude on the block, on campus, or in the office has ran through (Sexually).

I'm progressive enough to know that a woman is a sexual creature, just like a man. I understand that all women have sexual needs that they want to satisfy. However, I'm not trying to hear that it's okay for a woman to satisfy those needs any way and with anybody.

Nothing personally turns me off faster than a woman that

has been with everybody and has already done everything (I hate ho's).

Now I can just hear all of you "ho's" that are reading this saying, "I'm not a "ho". Men do it all of the time. When a man sleeps with a lot of women, he's a "playa" and gets a pat on his back. When a woman does it, she's a slut, "ho", and gets stoned. That's not fair." I only have one answer for that... "**HO**" please. Don't you dare sit up there and attempt to justify your "ho-ing". That sex in the city psychology doesn't work with me.

A ho is a ho (Period). If a man jumps off a building, while everyone is applauding and encouraging him on, would you jump off the building too? That's basically what you're saying. "Since he slept with one hundred women then I should be able to sleep with one hundred men." "**HO**" please! Don't blame a man or use his standards to justify your nasty behavior (remember I hate ho's). He's nasty and so are you. He's a ho and so are you. (PERIOD)

So far we looked at the negative side of being a "ho". Now lets define and examine the negative side of being a "bitch".

What is a bitch? Technically a "bitch" is a female dog, but that's not what we're talking about here. The slang definition of a "bitch" is a spiteful or overbearing woman" according to the American Heritage Concise Dictionary. I personally like that definition. I would also add that a "bitch" is an "arrogant, immature, and highly stubborn woman."

So the negative definition of a bitch that we will use is a "spiteful, arrogant, immature, stubborn, and overbearing woman (Got it).

A "bitch", is that woman who thinks the sun rises and sets on her. She's the woman that wants to sabotage someone's efforts at success and happiness. A "bitch", is that woman who never has anything positive to say, unless it involves her. Hopefully, you get the picture because the dynamics of what classifies one as a "bitch" are extended. I know you can easily give me at least ten scenarios of the "bitch". However, for time and page space we have to move on baby.

DivaGirl - How To Have A Good Man Find You

Positive (cool) Side

Like I said earlier, I believe nothing in and of itself is either good or bad. Even though the overwhelming majority of us view being a "bitch" or a "ho" as a bad and negative thing, everyone doesn't. We have to understand that there is also another way to look at and view anything. There are two sides to a coin and two sides of a bill.

So whether you agree with it or not, some people believe there is a positive definition of being a "ho". Some will say that a "ho" is a sexually liberated, open minded, and free spirited woman. Some will even say that a "ho" is a woman that is only doing what other women are afraid of doing. Many believe that a "ho" is only doing what all women really want to do. It's because of this philosophy that there are so many aspiring "ho's" in the world.

I find it discouraging that so many females believe a sexually liberated woman is someone that sleeps with both men and women. I would hate to believe a sexually liberated woman is someone that has several sexual partners at one time, or participates in orgies and menage-a-trois.

This whole Luke's peep show and Girls Gone wild culture is breeding ho's faster than a fat man can fill his plate in a buffet line. It's becoming an epidemic, with "ho's" everywhere.

We have little girls wanting to be "ho's". We have older women wanting to be "ho's", trying to get their groove back. We have some of the prettiest and sexiest women out here being the biggest "ho's" in the world. You definitely can't trust a big butt and pretty smile nowadays. This "ho" epidemic is serious. It's a damn shame. I mean first the Fat Boys broke up now this. There isn't anything to believe in anymore (Ha, ha).

Not only are there some that view being a ho as a cool and desirable thing. There are also some that think being a "bitch" is a good look. Unfortunately, too many of you lovely ladies think being a "bitch" is a sign of strength and power. There have been several high profile women that have proclaimed to the world to be the "biggest" and the "baddest" bitch there is.

I'm appalled that in a country that has been so disrespectful towards women that there are so many Black and Hispanic women calling themselves "bitches". Then again, I guess since they think that a "bitch" is an aggressive, strong, and no nonsense woman, that it's cool. It's definitely a sad day in Dodge, when our wives, mothers, sisters, and daughters no longer want to be "ladies" or "divas" anymore but "bitches" and "ho's". Daddy's little girl ain't little no mo.

It's Daddy's Fault

How does that precious and innocent little girl turn into that "bitch" and into that "ho". There are many angles we can take to look at this. I want to look at daddy's role. Since he is the cause of that little girl being here in the first place.

Daddy teaches his little girl how to trust, how to respect, and how to relate to the opposite sex. He provides for, protects her from, and points his little girl out into the world emotionally prepared.

When a father is absent or is not much of a father at all that little girl suffers. Her emotional needs for male (Mainly daddy's) affection, attention, and approval will go unfulfilled. She will attempt to fulfill those emotional needs with other men. She will do things to get the affection (just hold me), the attention (look at me), and the approval (you're pretty, smart, I love you) of men.

When a father is absent or isn't much of a father, a little girl will grow up lacking. She won't have the protective emotional covering that she requires, in order to grow and blossom into a woman. Many young girls and women in general, fall victim to the manipulative schemes of some men because there is no protective fence (wisdom and discernment) protecting their emotions. Their need for emotional satisfaction is so strong that they will allow any and every man into their world and "secret zone". The woman that lives without an emotional protective fence is usually a vulnerable and gullible woman.

The woman that lacks wisdom and discernment is usually that woman who "falls" in love the first week of *every relationship*. She's the woman that believes any and everything a man tells her is true. If a man gives her just a little affection (a hug), some attention (whispers sweet nothings) and his approval (you're beautiful), she'll give him everything (Her body, her bank card, etc).

Daddy's role is to breathe wisdom and the spirit of discernment into his little girl. Daddy is the reason why a little girl will grow up knowing the difference between love and lust. Daddy is the reason why his little girl is able to discern between a man's genuine interest and his "game".

Daddy can protect his little girl from that horny little boy, who only wants her body for his own sexual interest. Daddy can protect his little girl from that pimp, who wants her mind for his financial interest. Daddy can protect his little girl from the weak ass chump that wants to abuse and damage her self esteem. Daddy protect your little girl, she needs you.

When daddy is absent or is not much of a father that little girl may not be pointed out into the world with the emotional resolve needed to succeed in this world. Daddy lets his little girl know that she is intelligent, that she is capable of great things, and that she has a purpose in this male dominated business and political world. When daddy fails to point his little girl out into the world she may think that her only place in this world is to be a man's "plaything", a man's "prop", or a man's "possession".

I don't want to get too psychological and go too deep into this (that's another book), but daddy has an important role. Daddy has a very influential role in preparing his little girl for success and happiness, or setting her up for failure and despair.

Many women turn "bitch" because some man has emotionally scarred them. Understand, that no man is any more influential to a woman's development than her father. It's because of daddy that you now "need" a man to be so much in your life.

It's daddy fault. It's daddy fault. It's all daddy's fault!

When a man can't fulfill all of the extra responsibilities and expectations you placed on him, it hurts. You may feel unwanted, unattractive, and unappreciated because your man is not telling you and doing the things daddy "should" have done for you all along. As a result of all the disappointment and pain you've experienced, you now feel it's safer and more secure to be a "bitch". Being a bitch is your attempt at creating the protective fence that daddy was "supposed" to create for you.

Let me tell you something babygirl. Daddy's fence was to be one of wisdom, love, and discernment. The one you've created as a bitch is one of fear, anger, and resentment. Therefore, your fence is poisonous and dangerous to your property (your heart). Babygirl give the bitch thing up ASAP.

Many women turn "ho", because they crave daddy's touch, attention, and approval so bad that they are willing to trade and use their body to get it. That little girl, who allowed those four boys to run a "sex train" on her was looking for daddy's affection more than that sexual experience.

That woman, walking the streets with her ass all out for every man to see is looking for daddy's attention and approval. Daddy is leaving his little girl exposed and is slowly creating a victim. Daddy is creating a desperate and extremely demanding woman because of his absence and neglect. It's daddy's fault that we have so many "bitches" and "ho's".

Things Bitches & Ho's Do

For a little fun, I've created a quick "bitch" and "ho" checklist for you. I realize that the last subtitle may have caused some deep reflection and strong feelings. So now let's just have some lighthearted fun. This is also a little test/questionnaire, so answer the question for yourself. By the way, this is a test you definitely don't want to pass.

DivaGirl - How To Have A Good Man Find You

<u>Bitch & Ho Checklist</u>

- If no one in the office or in your class likes you:
  You are a bitch
- If you've slept with more than two guys from the office and it's only your second week on the job:
  You are a ho
- If you don't get along well with other women, it's not because women are catty, it's because:
  You are a bitch
- If you've sucked your man off and his man too:
  You are a ho
- If conflict and arguments turn you on:
  You are a bitch
- If you're in the clubs with a short skirt and no panties on:
  You are a ho
- If all of your girlfriends are bitches:
  You are a bitch
- If when a guy brings you over to his neighborhood and you already know his people:
  You are a ho
- If when you're gone no one misses you:
  You are a bitch
- If all it takes is an expensive car, some designers clothes, or some bling, bling to sleep with you:
  You are a ho
- If it's difficult for you to have a casual conversation with that brother who politely speaks to you on the bus, around campus, on the train, or in the elevator at work:
  You are a bitch
- If the number of men you've slept with surpasses your age:
  You are a ho

- If you're always feeling irritated, annoyed, or upset:
  - You are a bitch
- If all the dudes you sleep with never take you out on a date:
  - You are a ho
- If you can't seem to sustain a relationship for more than six months:
  - You are a bitch
- If all of your phone calls are booty calls:
  - You are a ho
- If you have sex for money or things
  - You are a ho
- If you have to "tell somebody off" at least once a day:
  - You are a bitch
- If people often say you're a "bitch" or "ho":

I'm sorry to inform you babygirl but you are a bitch you are a ho

I find the checklist to be hilarious, but it's straight up. Bitches aren't bitches by accident. A ho doesn't become a "ho" because she is misunderstood. "Bitches" and "ho's" are calculated and thought out. No one is born a "bitch" or a "ho". It's something that a person becomes.

"Bitches" and "ho's" are strong in the world. They are as strong as a STD or HIV. That's right, some of you who are reading this book are "bitches' and "ho's" (No disrespect intended). The good news is you can change. You can return back to the beautiful, noble, virtuous, and the special lady that you have been created to be. I sure hope so, because a "good" man doesn't connect or vibe with a "bitch" or a "ho". Now that I think about it. It won't make a difference anyway because to a "bitch" or "ho", a good man might be a "square" in her eyes.

DivaGirl - How To Have A Good Man Find You

Bitches & Ho's Don't Make Wives

I believe there is somebody for everyone. I believe that even "bitches" and "ho's" have their "soul mates" in the world. I believe that even a "bitch" or a "ho" can be evenly yoked with a man. I believe that there are several men that will welcome a "ho" or "bitch" into their world, with open arms. They are:

    1. **A "Pimp"**- He's in the business of employing and turning ho's out. A pimp is a ho's father figure

    2. **A "John"**- He is the sucker who pays to sleep with a "ho". He leases the Benz he can't afford, looks expensive in the club, but works three jobs just to keep a "ho's" expenses satisfied. He can also be called a "trick" because he spends to satisfy a "ho's" demands, even if he "really" doesn't have it like that.

    3. **A "Dog"**- He is the "no good" brother that women often associate with all men. A dog loves a good "bitch".

    4. **A "Playa"** – He is the dude that can care less. A playa has a woman for every purpose and his heart isn't with any of them. So a good "bitch" and a good "ho" serves a purpose.

    I hope you've noticed that not one of those men was the "good" man, or the "loving" husband that many of you desire in life.

    A quality man needs a quality woman and vice versa. Now don't get it twisted, a quality man will deal with a "bitch" or "ho" temporarily (Sexual purposes). However, for the long haul a "bitch" or a "ho" won't cut it for a quality brother looking for a quality relationship. It's not a good look for him.

    What man wants to come home and fight with his woman/ wife, after fighting other men all day long? What man wants to marry the woman all of his friend's and fraternity brothers have already slept with? It might not be fair babygirl, but this is bigger than you. You're not going to be able to sleep with every Tom and Dick then expect Harry to ask for your hand in marriage (Unless he doesn't know about the Toms and Dicks)

You're not going to be confrontational, stubborn, and overbearing, and think he's gonna run home to be with you at nights. I'm sorry baby, but that's how the ball bounces.

It doesn't matter how well you can cook or how good your sex may be. If you're a "bitch" or a "ho" you are gonna have problems in the long run. As soon as Mr. Lover, recognizes the "bitch" or "ho" in you, he's gonna have a problem with it. He might not even say anything up front, but it's coming sooner or later. He might not even verbalize his displeasure to you. But watch his actions. Watch his facial expressions in your company, notice his reluctance to introduce you to his family and friends, and watch the affection level drop. Nothing is worst for a man, than to find out that his woman is a "ho" (TRUST ME!). It brings a man down to have to deal with a "bitch" everyday. The world and its struggle is enough.

"Bitches" and "ho's" serve their purpose, especially a "ho". However, at the end of the day, it's not as the wife and the woman a man wants to bear his child.

Example: If you participate in a menagetrios with a man and another female, don't think for one second that the man is looking at you as a "wife". After his sight and vision returns from the lust (nut), you'll be a "ho" in his eyes. Take my word for it: And you could have been his "woman" going into it. No man wants to wife a "ho". No man wants to wife a "bitch". "Bitches" and "Ho's" don't make wives. *PLEASE BELIEVE ME!*

CONCLUSION

I hope I've made it clear that the "bitch " and "ho" look isn't fashionable. I hope I've shown you that it isn't fresh to express yourself in that manner. My goal is to help you maximize the woman in you. That way my brothers will be eager to step up their "games".

My efforts are in vain, if Ms. Bitch and Ms. Ho continue to impress and influence you. I'm sorry that your father wasn't much of a daddy. I'm sorry that daddy didn't give you what you needed emotionally as a little girl to grow into a healthy woman. It really is unfortunate that you are still battling childhood "needs" and "issues". We will continue to work through them all. Just continue to read along babygirl.

There is so much I want to support you with. I'm not about to support your "bitchy" attitude and disposition. I'm not about to co-sign on your "ho-ing". You are better than that. I expect more of you. Maybe daddy was a sucker, but I'm not. You will become more messing around with me. Bet that!

Besides you have so much to accomplish and achieve in this world. The best of your best is needed. There are a thousand times more of you, to be lived, and expressed. So destroy everything that seeks to destroy you.

I hope you understand that an assertive woman will be respected. Any man can respect and appreciate a sensual or sexual woman. It's cool to be a woman with a voice, a woman in tune with her sensuality. However, the "bitch" and "ho" must die. Do me a favor baby. Help me to eliminate the "bitches" and "ho's" from among us. If you're one of the "bitches" or "ho's" we are looking for, you better change ASAP. Me and all of the "ladies" and "divas" of the world are coming after you.

It's the "bitches" and "ho's", working along side the "niggas" and "suckers" that are killing the community. We've stopped experiencing the beauty and power of love and romance, between the man and the woman because of them and their bullshit.

I will admit it. Daddy has crippled many of us. He has failed and left his little girl vulnerable in a cold, cold world. Unfortunately, life goes on. Now daddy's little girl is a "bitch" now she's a "ho". Damn world, daddy's little girl ain't little no mo.

CHAPTER 5

RELATIONSHIPS 101:   JUST IN
CASE YOU FORGOT

"It's the simple things we complicate that make the difficult things seem impossible."
Rich Gilmore

INTRODUCTION

We are now about to get down to the nitty gritty. One of the main reasons why you paid money for this book was because you wanted something in return. You wanted to learn how to maximize your womanhood. You wanted to learn how to have a good man find you. Staying true to the purpose of this book, and being the good businessman that I am, I will give you what you paid money for.

The remainder of the book will be all about *relationships*. It's going to be all about how that good man is going to find you. I will also give you some advice on how to bring the good out of the man you have now. Be clear, I don't have any steps or any mind games for you to play (Read those other books). All I have is the truth and principles. All I have to give you is some wise advice.

Remember, it's perfectly okay for you to disagree with me. I think it's important that you always think for yourself and make your own judgements. I only ask that you listen and consider what it is that I'm really saying (seek understanding), before you make a judgement.

I understand that there are different strokes for different folks. I realize that my position is one as a young, heterosexual, African American man. I accept and can live with the fact that I may offend certain groups of people with my words and perspective..

The beauty of this country is that we have a Constitutional right to speak our minds and to express our views, in a law abiding way. Therefore, I will continue to speak and do what I do, the only way I know how to do it. Keep in mind, my motivation isn't controversy but love and positive change. So to any groups that I may offend...I'm sorry, but it is what it is.

Relationship Basics

Marriage, parenthood, family, friendship, business partnerships, all share a common thread. They are all relationships. If you really want to get technical, everything in life is a relationship. If a relationship is one's connection and relation to a person or thing, then everything in life is a relationship.

There are three major elements that man must relate to in a positive and productive way, if he is to succeed in life. So as a woman there are three elements that must come together for you, in order to be effective in life

Three Power Elements
People
The Environment (nature, earth)
Material Possessions

The faster you come to grips with your connection to these three elements, the sooner your life will feel complete, meaningful, and whole.

Connectors

In addition to there being three major elements to life, there are three power connectors that connect one to the elements.

Three Power Connectors
Love- connects you to people
Money- connects you to material things
Breath- connects you to the environment

Once again, here I go covering the basics and fundamentals again. I'm not trying to insult your intelligence in any way. But how many of us complicate and confuse the simple things in life? We make everything difficult, and take so much way too seriously. So I'm going back to the drawing board. Just in case you forgot or were never taught the things I will share, I'm going to cover the basics. Is that alright with you sweetheart?

We are connected to people because of love (ego, fear, and hate separates). We are connected to material things because of money. Obviously, we are connected to our environment (earth) because of the breath we breathe in and out of our bodies. Don't make the mistake of thinking that you are connected to your environment, because of your mother and father. As much as that may appear to be true that is not the case. Oh, you don't believe me, then think about this?

What would happen if you lose your father or mother? After grieving a bit, life would go on, right? Now what would happen if you lost your breath? If you weren't resuscitated, it would be a wrap for you. So understand that love connects you to people, money to things, and your breath to the environment.

Love, money, and breath, are your connectors to other people, material things (cars, homes, clothes, etc) and the environment. Now don't start limiting your thinking. Please believe that money will connect you to people. I don't know why it is, but as soon as you get some money, you also get a lot of "friends" and "family members".

Understand that to some degree, money can sustain your connection to the environment. That's why if you don't have any now make it your business to get some health insurance. Make sure you are covered.

Keep in mind that *love* keeps you connected to people long term (Live in love). Understand that *money* keeps you connected to material things (Get money). Never ever forget that it's your *breath* that keeps you connected to the environment (Breathe, relax, enjoy yourself)

Why Is It Important?

If you've noticed anything about me so far, I hope that you recognized I'm a very methodological fella. Knowing that I hope you understand why I mentioned and discussed the power elements and the power connectors.

Well for starters, I told you that the rest of the book would be all about relationships and how you are to connect with that good man right? So I had to lay down the law, before I started arresting your false beliefs and crazy assumptions.

Remember, I don't have a "ten steps to getting married" or a "101 ways to pleasing your man" strategy to give you. I believe every woman and every man has their own personality and style. That's why, I don't believe in those silly games or tricks. They don't work the same for everyone. The only things that work for everyone is the *truth* and *principle.*

If I throw two balls up into the air, and James your boyfriend throws two balls up into the air as well, the principle of gravity will bring both of our balls back down to earth. The principle of gravity will work on my balls, just like it would on James' balls. The only difference would be that my balls are bigger (Get it).

I remember one of my former girlfriends would read Cosmopolitan magazine like it was the Bible. She would take the advice and follow all of those bullshit (pardon the language) techniques like they were the Ten Commandments or something. She was always surprised when the tricks or techniques wouldn't work out on me like they described in the magazine. She couldn't comprehend why I didn't like my nipple pinched, when the magazine said it would drive me crazy.

I never understood why she would go to a magazine to find out how I felt, or to find out what I wanted. She could have saved herself the four dollars or whatever she paid for it a month, and just asked me. Maybe if she had asked me, we would still be together (I need to give her a call).

I think Cosmo, Ebony, or any other magazine you may read is your business. I don't have anything personal against anyone of those magazines (I really don't). I'm not telling you what to read or not read. You are a grown ass woman. You are entitled to spend your money however you see fit. I'm just thankful that you picked up my book (Thank you baby).

Just remember you won't be learning any new *steps*. I want you to feel free to be who you are. I want you to get the most out of your relationship. So remember, the first set of principles we've discussed, love to people, money to things, and breathe to life.

Relationship Fundamentals

If I were to ask you, what are the keys to a successful relationship, what would you say? Before you answer the question, keep in mind I like to keep things simple. Now give me three things.

     1. _____
     2. _____
     3. _____

Did you answer communication, trust, and sharing? Regardless, if you did or did not, you weren't wrong. There are no right or wrong answers here.

I want us to look at three more ingredients to a relationship, that are often over looked. I often hear people say that communication is the key to a relationship. I would agree, communication is key. However, I think that there is more to it than just communicating. Besides, when most people say communication they're only referring to "talking".

When I say communication is the key to a relationship, I'm referring to the talking, the touching, the thinking, and the believing that is exchanged. I'm referring to more than just the verbal exchange. As a result, I think that communication is key. I would also say that respect, truth, and desire run deeper.

I think that respect, truth, and desire, are three forces that go unnoticed because they are so silent in relationships. I want you to follow along and seriously take into consideration these three potent forces. Respect, truth, and desire, are what determines success in a relationship.

Respect

How well do you communicate with someone that you don't respect? Think about someone that you have little to no respect for right now (ex-boyfriend, coworker, etc). You have someone in mind right? Okay, now just think about the thoughts you have about that person. Think about how you affectionately interact with this person. Think about how you talk to that person. Think about how you talk about that person to others.

Now reverse the whole process. Do it for someone that you do respect (parent, friend, role model). See the difference? The quality of the communication you have with that person is much healthier.

There was a reason why the first chapter of this book was entitled, "All men are good". If you are to get the most out of this book you have to respect men. I know that a lot of males are disrespectful towards women. However, you still have to find it in your heart again to respect all men.

If you do come across a disrespectful male, realize that he has a "problem". Remember, it doesn't have to become your problem. There is nothing in life that says just because someone is disrespectful towards you that you have to return the disrespect. Please believe that regardless if you are a lady or not there will be some "nigga", or "asshole" that will show his ass out of disrespect.

Many times men are disrespectful towards women not because of the woman. Most of the time males are disrespectful because of their manhood (He's a sucker). So if you run into a knucklehead, keep it moving, shake it off, or firmly put him in his place, if need be. However, never fall victim to the disrespect cycle (You're too fly for that).

Respect is essential to effectively communicating and relating to others. Think about how some White people in this country treated Black people, who they didn't respect. Have you noticed just how disrespectful men and women are towards one another today? How are we to effectively communicate and resolve the pettiness between us without respect? Without respect, how are you to deal with and accept the differences between you and your man? Respect is key.

Truth

People are always talking about the issue of trust when they talk about relationships. Women say, "You can't trust no man. A man is always gonna be a man (Whatever that means). Men say, "Women are sneaky and you can't trust no bitch."

With all of this name calling and false thinking, is it any wonder why we don't see the truth anymore. Now back to the communication factor. Let's say that you and I talk a lot, meaning we consistently communicate (talk). Yet, throughout our conversations all I do is lie to you. To add insult to injury all you ever do is catch me out there in my lies. Will you trust me? Remember we are *communicating*. You wouldn't trust me as far as you can throw me, right? Exactly. Truth is the prerequisite of trust. Trust is built on truth.

Principle #10 - You won't trust that which is dishonest.

Now I want you to think about something. If you don't respect men, you and I meet and decided to build a quality relationship. How are we gonna effectively communicate when you don't respect my position (perspective) as a man, or trust my character? Do you think you would treat me differently because I wrote this book? Hell No! I would receive the same treatment as the next man...sooner or later.

Common sense would say that as long as I'm respectable and honest with you, there "shouldn't" be any problems, right? **Wrong!** Now let me show you why.

Principle #11 - Generalities supercedes specificity.

If a White store owner doesn't respect or trust Black people. If that store owner thinks we are all thieves and criminals, especially those of us who wear urban sportswear. What would happen if I walked into his store, wearing a sweat suit, durag, and fitted cap? Keep in mind I'm a respectable brother and I honestly want to purchase something from within the store. What would happen to me? Better yet, how would they treat me within this store? You better believe they would have a flashlight cop (security guard), a surveillance camera, and a sales clerk following my ass around until I either purchased something or left the store. Understand babygirl that until you respect and trust **all** men, you're not gonna freely and effectively communicate with **a** man. You won't even effectively communicate with **your man** for that matter (You'll always be suspicious).

DivaGirl - How To Have A Good Man Find You

Desire

How can I get you to do something that you don't want to do? I "can't " (curse word). It's impossible for me to get you to do something that you don't want to do. I can hear you now, "Of course you can". But that's your false thinking again.

Principle #12 - People only do what they have a desire for.

In order to get someone to act you have to create a desire for that person. The two most common ways to create a desire for someone is by *asking* (willfully) someone to do something, or by *telling* (forcefully) someone to do something.

If I wanted my niece to clean up her room, I could politely ask her, "Keniya, can you please clean up your room?" I can also tell her forcefully, "Keniya, get your ass in there and clean up that room, right now." Either way you look at it I'm creating a desire for her to act. One method may be more effective than another. Then again that depends on the situation. Understand babygirl that without a desire, whether by will or force, there is no action.

$10 Million dollar question
- So how does this relate to communicating?
$100 Million dollar answer
- It has everything to do with it.

If you don't have a desire to understand another person, you won't listen to or take into consideration their point of view. Now you tell me something. How do you get to know someone, without ever listening to them speak?

It happens all of the time, people have no desire to understand another person then get angry because they fight over simple misunderstandings. People don't have the motivation to know the truth, then they wonder why they are so confused about things. People have no desire to change then complain because they feel like they are in a "rut" with their relationships and life.

DivaGirl - How To Have A Good Man Find You

Wisdom gem* If you want to understand where your man is coming from; if you want to share your world with him, then "desire" to listen to him. "Desire" to make some changes, some adjustments, and watch your life improve. "Desire" to know the truth instead of protecting your opinions and watch your soul be free.

Desire is the heart of everything. Without desire there is no action. Without action (cause), there are no results (effects). Therefore, if you want to effectively communicate and have a successful relationship with a man then *desire* to respect all men, *desire* to honestly deal with yourself, and never forget to *desire* understanding.

Relationships

As with everything there are levels and degrees to relationships. Some relationships are stronger and run deeper than others. For discussion sake I will only talk about the relationships that will satisfy your desire to meet that good man. There are generally three levels or dimensions of a male/female relationship.

Casual
Platonic
Monogamous

Casual

I know this might be a little too elementary for you but continue to follow along anyhow (There's a method to all of this). A casual relationship is basically a relationship in which you occasionally date someone. It's a relationship where you'll probably see the other person once a month. You hardly ever talk to this person, unless it's to hook up and to meet somewhere. A casual relationship can take on many forms but none of them are that deep. Love and romance are not a part of this relationship.

However, sex can become a part of this relationship. Usually it is an ingredient in this union.

Due to human nature and the law of motion, casual relationships don't last that long before they are forced into change. Over time a casual relationship will either progress into something more, or dissolves back into separation. When you're in a casual relationship with a man, you barely speak to him, you see him once every full moon, and you invest little to nothing into the relationship. However, sooner or later something is gonna have to give with you all's situation.

By design, casual relationships from a "romantic" perspective are meant to be short term in nature. Have you noticed that when you casually see someone, especially if the relationship is sexual, after a while you'll want more, or somehow the relationship just dissipates?

Think about that dude who you thought sex was good. Now for whatever reason, he could've been another woman's man, or you were creeping out on your man. For whatever reason, (there are many) the relationship was casual. You two would hook up once in a while, and sex every blue moon. What happened to that relationship? He either became your man and more than a casual sex partner, or he just fell off of the planet right? Remember babygirl, casual "romantic" relationships are short lived.

Wisdom gem* It might not be a good idea to give a casual relationship that which you would give a marriage.

Platonic

We all know what a platonic relationship is. It's the "buddy, buddy, friend, friend" relationship. It's a relationship that surpasses the physical. In a platonic relationship sex isn't exchanged. Platonic friends are actually "soul mates".

Contrary to popular mythology, "soul mates" are people that connect in thought, desire, values, and personalities. Platonic relationships between a men and a women I find special. In a "sex crazed" society, I think it's "heavenly" when a man and a woman connects that way. For a man and woman to meet on a pure soul level is unfortunately a rare occurrence.

In a perfect world we would all establish platonic relationships with people before we take things to another level with them. The whole "friends before lovers" concept is a powerful notion. Unfortunately, we don't have the time anymore to *"get to know someone"*.

We have to work two jobs, take classes at night, tend to our family responsibilities, watch four to six hours of TV a day, and just do all the other things that take up every waking minute. I mean who has the time to talk and share your experiences, goals, and values with someone special anymore. Who wants to sit out in a park and just talk to a friend nowadays? Especially when we're paper chasing and lusting after "stuff".

We are so confused and contaminated in our thinking. We think sleeping with a platonic friend is alright. I've been guilty of saying that infamous line myself, "Nah, it's not that serious. We are "just"(supposedly meaning platonic) friends."

Ladies be warned. It's difficult for a man to say "no" to sex, but it's very easy for a man to say "no" to a serious committed relationship. I actually believe that women hold the sexual authority in a relationship (I know brothers are mad I'm saying this).

Look at it this way. In order to have sex a man has to enter into your body. Now if you don't let him in it ain't going down. He can beg and plead all he wants. But until you let him in he won't get in (unless by rape). Think about this. No one can enter into your house unless they have a key or if you let them in (excluding a break in). Some of you ladies have given keys to everybody in your neighborhood. Some of y'all leave your door wide open all day long.

It's important that you understand a "platonic" relationship doesn't involve sexual intercourse of any kind (oral, vaginal, anal, etc). Once sex is in the equation a relationship is no longer "platonic". It's sad that we have allowed sex to ruin many a "platonic" friendship. I believe we do so because we don't know how to communicate without sex.

Just know, a platonic friend is a true "soul mate", someone you have connected to on a meaningful level. So honor and respect the beauty of a platonic connection. Sex is also a beautiful thing just do things the "right" way.

Monogamous

I'm sure all of you ladies can tell me what a monogamous relationship is. I only question if you know how deep and layered a monogamous relationship really is. I doubt if many of you ladies do know how deep monogamy is. I say that because I've noticed many women are quick to "jump" into a monogamous relationship. A monogamous relationship, on the surface, is a relationship in which two people commit to exclusively only seeing each other. It's the relationship that we all know about. It's the relationship that many of us want at the end of the day.

Unknowingly, many people rush into a monogamous relationship without an understanding of the principles that govern the dimensions of this type of union. I think if we all knew about these laws people would exercise more wisdom and patience, before they commit themselves to *one* person.

I actually believe many of us are conditioned to believe in "marriage", as this ideal situation. As a result, we rush into monogamous relationships in our pursuit of the ideal situation or relationship. I also think that marriage is a great situation, but there is more to life and relationships than *marriage*. (TRUST ME!)

If we will open up and appreciate wherever we are, I think more of us would be at peace. I think we would also enjoy ourselves more. Then our relationships wouldn't be so strained. Monogamy isn't something that we "should" take lightly. There are laws we must obey if that relationship is to succeed. There are laws that must be obeyed for a monogamous relationship to **flow**.

DivaGirl - How To Have A Good Man Find You

Three Supreme Laws Of A Monogamous Relationship:
The law of agreement
The law of exchange
The law of growth

Law of Agreement

This law states that if you and Mr. Lover are to become monogamous, you have to be one not ~~two~~ individuals. The law states that you two must have a clear understanding of each other (Know your man). It states that you two must have the same objective for the relationship (He wants you and you want him). This law says that you two must be headed in the same direction, in life as a team.

Law of Exchange

This law states that nothing comes from nothing and that something comes from something. The law states that the things you and Mr. Lover Lover want out of the relationship must be the things you two are willing to put into the relationship. This law says that you must sow before you reap. This law says that whatever qualities you want out of the relationship (love, happiness, fulfillment), must first be given to your mate and to the relationship. You don't get peace from confusion, happiness from jealousy, and you definitely don't get love from lust (You feel me).

Example: If you and Mr. Lover want to get married, invest partnership, honesty, and commitment into you all's relationship (sow marriage).

DivaGirl - How To Have A Good Man Find You

Law of Growth

This law states that everything physical is moving and experiencing the dynamics of change. This law applies to your physical body, your feelings, and your world as you currently know. All physical elements are changing just as the earth rotates. It is all a necessary function of evolution and growth. All things must change in order to evolve.

Now let me ask you a few questions Ms. Lady. How can you determine if you and Romeo are in agreement? How can you determine if you and Romeo are committed to giving your all to the relationship? How can you determine if you and Romeo are both willing to experience the changes and challenges of life together? Pretty lady, how can you determine all of that... in *two weeks*?

Why are you so willing to jump into a monogamous relationship, giving up so much, so damn fast? I believe you may be rushing into committed relationships so fast because of two reasons: Desperation and Sex

Principle #13 - Desperate people are radical and reckless with their behavior.

I am never surprised by some of the things I see and hear from desperate people. It's out of desperation that you move so fast, giving up the booty before you even get a brother's last name. To the natural eye you look like a "ho" because you gave up that "sweet stuff" two hours into the relationship. No one can see that beneath the surface you are trying to fulfill an emotional need, more than just a sexual or physical one.

I have had my own share of experiences with women that wanted a monogamous relationship with me, only after *two weeks* into the relationship. I'll never understand how a woman could want me to be her man when all she really knows about me is my name, where I live, or any of that basic job interview information. I

102

know that I'm a good catch, but **damn**. Take it easy ladies (I'm frontin` hard right now)

Wisdom gem* In order for you to "know" what it is that you like, you first have to "know".

So be easy, relax, and take your time to get to know a man, especially before you open your sexual doors and let him into your body. First take the time to find out if he's "worthy" to have some of you (unless your goods are cheap), before you give him some.

So keep in mind, there's the casual connection (short term), there is the platonic connection (soul mate), and then there's the monogamous (serious) connection. I hope you realize that if you really want to develop a solid relationship it's important that you experience all three connections.

For instance, you meet someone that gets your attention and you find him interesting. Y'all casually date (no sex) for a period of time and really start to vibe with each other. Then, you two start to connect on the soul level developing a respectable and special friendship (I know it might be hard at this point but still no sex). Then, after some time, based on your own situation and judgment you two decide to make it exclusive. Now is the time for you two to become monogamous and share your world with each other. Now it's okay to do what you do (sexually). Just make sure you do it safely. At this point the relationship will be standing on solid grounds. A true friendship of respect, trust, and desire is built, and the relationship is now built to last.

*Don't get it twisted for one second, there is no standard length of time with this. It can all happen in two weeks (which is rare), or in two months. Each relationship is unique and special. But building any relationship is a process of principle.

DivaGirl - How To Have A Good Man Find You

Relationship Styles

Earlier, I mentioned that I believe everyone has their own personality and their own style. As a result, I also believe that when two individuals with their own personalities and relationship styles come together, a bigger picture is created.

In my evaluations, I've come to discover that women have seven relational styles. When these styles partner with a complimenting energy, a new dynamic evolves.

Seven Relational Styles Of A Women

Mother- She's nurturing, controlling, a problem solver, she loves to run things in the relationship.

Sister- She's warm, friendly, and looks for companionship more than a lover.

Daughter- She's extremely needy, highly sensitive, demands direction from her man.

Girl- She's immature, looking for immediate gratification, and unstable. She's often very materialistic and easy to please with "stuff".

Woman- She's mature, well balanced, and stable. She's ready for marriage and family

Bitch- She's overbearing, stubborn, and self centered

Ho- She's unfaithful, promiscuous, and wild

Seven Relationship Dynamics

"Mother" & "Son"

For those of you women that predominately function as a "mother" in a relationship. Meaning you are a caregiver, you love to solve your man's problems, and you love to groom a man to your satisfaction. In order for a relationship to work for you, you need a man whose relational style is one of a "son". You need someone who will be dependent on you for help. You need someone with a lot of problems that you can solve. In essence, you basically need a "project", someone you can work on to make "good".

I think this is one of the two most common relationship dynamics. The woman that lets her man "live" off of her is a mother. The woman that is always working to change her man is a mother. The mother relational style seeks the "son" relational compliment for fulfillment and satisfaction.

"Daughter" & "Father"

The woman that has a "daughter" relational style, meaning she is extremely emotionally needy, she is highly sensitive, and depends on her man for direction. This woman needs a father, someone that will take care of her many needs and lead her through life. This dynamic is the second most common relational style for women today.

Women that lacked the emotional fulfillment of their biological father will often search for him in their relationships later on. This woman usually wants her man to pay her bills, buy all of her clothes, tell her what she can and can not do (be possessive). She is looking to be treated like "daddy's little girl". Women with the "relational" style of a "daughter" seek their "father" in their man.

"Sister" & "Brother"

The "sister" relational style is very warm, friendly, and seeks a friend more than a lover with her man. She enjoys conversation more than lovemaking. This style needs the "brother" compliment to be fulfilled in life. A "sister" and "brother" are harmonious together and make each other happy. "Sisters" are great at establishing "platonic" relationships.

"Woman" & "Man"

This is personally my favorite relational style and dynamic in the world. A "woman" is a mature, stable, and prepared style.

This is the style that is positioned to go to the highest level (Marriage). A "woman" only connects to a "man".

A "woman", is too much for anyone else. A "son" will feel she's too demanding, a "father" will feel that she's too independent, and a "brother" will feel that she's moving too fast. When God created Adam and Eve, he created a "man" and a "woman" to run his earth. The "woman" style is the healthiest among the seven. In fact, my whole objective with this book is to help you mature and transform into the "woman" style. That way, you will magnetically be attracted to the "man". The "woman" and "man" relationship is the eighth wonder of the world.

The last two relational styles and dynamics the "bitch and dog" and "ho and pimp", I've already covered in the previous chapter. Therefore, I won't discuss it again. So let's move on.

Now do you better understand why you seem to always run into and connect with the "scrub"? You're a "mother", and subconsciously you think and desire a man that will satisfy your relational style. To my "daughters", do you now understand why you keep looking for a man that can "do" for you?

Your relational style determines the energy, or "cause" you set into motion. That cause, will reflect your "effect" or relational compliment.

I would like to think that all of this was so simple and rational but it's not. In reality, your relational style is a combination of several of the styles I mentioned. During a relationship you will wear different hats at different times.

That's why, if you initially connect with a "son", he'll frustrate you with his immaturity and instability when you put on your "woman" hat. A "son", will irritate you when he can't satisfy your dependency, if you put on your "daughter" hat. The key to all of this is to respect Godly universal principles.

Principle #14 - People are perfectly who they are but imperfectly who we want them to be.

DivaGirl - How To Have A Good Man Find You

Understand babygirl, your relational style and needs will change throughout the course of a relationship. You will go from "mother" to "daughter" or from "sister" to "woman", all within the span of your relationship.

I would love to see the "bitch" and "ho" relational styles transform into a "woman". Just realize that you are always changing and going through transitions. So don't start trippin` out on your mate when you realize your desires are changing. You might just be going through your cycle (Not just menstrual).

If the change is going on within you, why would you be upset with your man? He doesn't feel what you are feeling... when you feel it. Be realistic and fair, people are perfect being who they are.

Keep in mind that it's up to you. You determine the "style" and "quality" of connection you will make with a man, based on the vibration, energy, and needs you send out into the world.

I would now like to ask you a simple question based on what we just covered. If you want to have a "good" **man** find you, what type of energy must you send out? What relational style must you express predominately? That's right, you need to send out *"good"* vibrations, and you need to be a **"woman"**. It all sounds simple and it is simple when you understand the mathematics and science behind it. I want you to realize that above all of this "mother", "daughter", and "woman" relational stuff, that you just have to be *yourself.* That will be the most impressive and effective thing to do anyway.

You never want to "try" to be anything that you're not ready to become. It will only frustrate you and you'll come off as a "phony". Be positive and loving towards yourself, towards men, and in relationships. Good things will only happen to and for you. **I PROMISE!.**

CONCLUSION

So as you can now see relationships are all principle based. Whether you obey the principles or not, they still govern our affairs. You don't have to respect the principle of gravity, but jump off a building and watch what happens. Even if we are ignorant or disobedient of these laws and principles, they will still govern. So be wise and respect that which is greater than you. Use the principles and advice in this chapter and book to your advantage. Don't just read this book as entertainment. Allow it to educate and inspire you to change. You can have it all.

CHAPTER 6

SEX AIN'T LOVE: OR WHATEVER WE CALL IT

"Do you love me?"

Woman before, during, and after sex

"What's love got to do with it?"

Tina Turner

INTRODUCTION

How is it going babygirl? I hope that you've been enjoying yourself with the book so far. I hope you've learned something new about yourself, about men, and about relationships. We are now about to discuss three of the most misunderstood and undervalued energies in the world, sex, romance, and love. I do have some good news. After this chapter you will be a whole lot clearer on the dynamics of sex, romance, and love?

In the past, have you ever misunderstood sex for love? I mean, did you ever have a strong sexual connection with a man and mistake it for love? Did you think he loved you and you loved him just because he was able to make your toes curl? Honestly think about it. I'm quite sure that you have made that mistake at some point in your past.

Have you ever mistaken romance for love? I mean, have you ever had strong emotional feelings for someone and called it "love". Think about the times when the thought, or sound of his voice, made you melt. Think about that time when you couldn't wait to see and talk to him. Did you call that "love"? Did you think you were falling in "love"? I bet you did. That's why when that "phase" of the relationship changed you thought and maybe even said, "I'm not "in love" with Tyrone anymore." The truth is you were never in love with Tyrone sweetheart.

This is gonna be another in your face, "let's get your mind right" chapter. I bet after you read this chapter you will know more about the forces of sex, romance, and love like you never have before.

Do remember, if you find this book to be entertaining and enlightening buy two or more copies and give them as gifts to the women you really care about (Spread the love). I had to slip some promotion in there on you.

I Love Having Sex!

Sexual intercourse is a wonderful force and experience that is misused and undervalued today. People have sex for every reason under the sun. If I drive a nice car... I can have sex. If I say all of the right things to a lovely lady... I can have sex (Eventhough I'm married). If I show a woman a pleasant evening... I can have sex. If the Yankees when another championship... I can have sex. If I write a book... I can have sex. (It's true I can)

We make it our business to find new ways and more reasons to get our sex on. Unfortunately, with all of the sexing going on in the world the majority of us don't know what sex really is.

Sex is more than getting a nut (Having an orgasm). Sex is more than a position or style. Sex is more than 101 ways to satisfying your mate. Sex is a force, a natural power in the earth. Sexual energy is a very powerful force. It must be exercised with special care or someone can get hurt.

I truly believe that people "should" have a license before

they start having sex. Think about it. You need a driver's license before you can legally operate a motor vehicle. Why not have someone get a sex license before they can start legally having sex. I guess that's where the whole sex before marriage practice came into play.

Let me ask you a question. Do you enjoy spending money? Do you enjoy going shopping? If you have children, would you like it if I were to take you and your kids shopping to the stores of your choice? Chances are you would not only like that, you would love it. You might even think about giving me "some".

Now, do you enjoy paying your credit card bills? Do you enjoy having to pay for dry cleaning or car repairs? Do you enjoy seeing your kids ruin those sneakers and clothes you spent money on? Would you like it if after I took you and your kids out shopping, I started acting like I owned you? Would you like that? Of course you wouldn't. You would then probably regret having gave me "some", even though it was good. (I'm not frontin' here)

What I did with the first set of questions was give you some benefits. Then, I gave you some responsibilities and circumstances to deal with. Obviously you enjoyed and welcomed the benefits. But you would rather do without the responsibilities and circumstances. It's not because you're irresponsible or immature. We would all take the benefits and pass on the responsibilities in life. It's because we all enjoy pleasure more than we do pain (unless you are a pain freak).

Principles #15 – People look to obtain pleasure and avoid pain.

We all enjoy the pleasures of sex. What's better than some spine tingling, sheet clinching, and sweat pouring sex. Anybody who has ever really "did the damn thing" understands what I'm talking about. For those of you inexperienced rookies that haven't been touched by the "sexualizer" yet, y'all need to come on in, while the getting is still good.

Seriously speaking we can all testify to the pleasures a

good sexual experience can bring. It can relieve tension and bring you closer to someone. When done properly, it's actually good for your health and overall well being (That's cool right).

However, in the care of a lustful, irresponsible, and immature person sex can cause far more pain than good. A STD is *PAIN*, HIV is *PAIN*, and an unwanted pregnancy and dislike for your baby's mother or father, is *PAIN*. The emotional, mental, and physical damage that sex, when misused can cause, is devastating.

We are all familiar with the numbers and rising statistics on the spread of STD's and HIV. We all are participants or have witnessed the "babymother/babyfather" episode. However, we don't examine the emotional or mental repercussions that sex can have on us.

Don't get me wrong, I love to have sex just like the next person, if not more. I'm not about to sit up here and make sex look like a bad, dirty, or a painful experience. However, I do have a new and ever growing appreciation for the sex force. I now believe that sex can only "truly" prosper in the hands of the loving, the responsible, and the mature. Until there are two loving, mature, and responsible parties, I would recommend that you wait before having sex. (It's killing me to even say it)

Trust me, I know it's hard to go cold turkey, especially when you're accustomed to getting it on. So if you have to go visit your local sex shop and make a few personal purchases. Take this time to really get to know yourself (seriously). Find out and explore what it is that you like. Find out what floats your boat. If you don't know what gets you off, how is Mr. Lover supposed to know?

Sex is natural and beautiful, but not when it's done lustfully (I don't care for him), irresponsibly (practice safe sex), or immaturely (let's get an abortion; it ain't my baby). Sex is actually like money and drugs.

Sex is like money because when in the proper hands, it can make the world a better place. However, when in the wrong hands sex can destroy. Sex is like a drug because it can become addictive.

Sex can also be used to heal a body or to cause sickness and disease to one. So realize sex is a very dynamic thing.

Sex Force

By design we are sexual creatures with hormones that generate sexual energy and desires within us. Remember without desire there is no action.

Therefore, it's perfectly okay and natural for you to have sexual desires (I don't care what "they" say).

If we didn't have a desire for sex, no one but Adam and Eve would be here. If it wasn't for sex, I wouldn't have been able to write this book, and you definitely wouldn't be reading it. If it weren't for sex, our behinds wouldn't be here (That's real). So let's give up the whole "religious sex as taboo", theory.

Principle #16 - Whatever we fear becomes stronger whatever we face becomes weaker.

For far too long we've been afraid of sex when we need to embrace and appreciate its force. I think the reason why there are so many of us walking around confused, uneducated, and intimated by sex, is because those who "should" have the answers are too afraid of the questions.

The "church" runs like a coward from the issues of sex. The "school" makes a half ass effort in answering our curiosity. Most parents leave it up to the "church" and the "school" to educate their children on their sexuality and bodies. That's why there is so much chaos and destruction, as a result of our misuse and abuse of sex.

It's sad that little girls are growing up ashamed of their bodies and ignorant of feminine hygiene. There is a little girl struggling right now with her sexuality. Unfortunately, Pastor "Know it all", mommy, and Mrs. Brown, (her sexual education teacher), can't help her out.

They can't help her mainly because they are struggling with their sexuality also. Pastor "Get money", doesn't know if it's a woman or a little boy that he wants sexually. Mommy doesn't know if it's a man or her friend Pam that she wants to be with. Mrs. Brown is restricted by law to remain "politically correct". So she's handcuffed with a muzzle on her mouth.

Maybe there wouldn't be so many single mothers, homosexuals, bisexuals, molestation, and STD's in the church, if Pastor "Say what sounds good", would grow some balls and show them. Maybe if Pastor "Hypocrite", would start addressing the needs of the people and stopped talking about religious concepts that little boy or girl wouldn't be so damned curious and confused.

I appreciate the effort our educational system makes towards educating our youth on sex and safe sex measures. I'm furious and outraged at that powerless "church". My problem is with the so called "men and women of God", who refuse to tell the truth and be truth in this real world we are living in. It's because of the "church" and religion that sex is now so taboo.

I actually stopped going to church because the people and Pastor were so "phony" in my opinion. There I was "trying" (those were my "trying" days) to get right and live how they said I "should" live (which turned out to be a bunch of "BS"). Meanwhile, as I'm there getting my "worship" on, every girl in the pew was trying to get their "freak" on with me. Only thing I wasn't in the club checkin` for the ladies, I was there in church searching for God. But the worst part of it all was there were more sissies in the damn church, than in San Francisco and Boys Town put together. I'm telling you I was disgusted babygirl, and that's why I don't go to church to find God anymore (Especially since he lives in me).

The good news is, I'm here to tell you what the "church", "school system", and what your parents have been too afraid of, or ignorant of themselves, and didn't tell you. I will give it to you real, confronting you if need be. Just keep in mind my desire isn't to offend you. My motivation is to love. It's all love babygirl.

Masculinity & Femininity Forces

Like I've stated earlier, there is a masculine and a feminine nature and energy in the universe. There is also a masculine and feminine sexual force in the universe. By design the masculine sex force resides predominately in males. Males produce testosterone to generate their sexual energy. The masculine sex force is proactive, assertive, and seeks its feminine compliment, by nature for a complete expression. Therefore, it's perfectly natural and normal for a man to sexually desire a woman.

It's perfectly normal babygirl for a man to proactively and assertively pursue you for sexual relations. So don't trip when a man propositions you for sex (It's what we do). Especially, if the first things you introduced him to are your juicy ass and titties.

A man's sexual energy causes him to get an erection that is designed to penetrate a WOMAN'S womb (Not another man's butt hole). A woman produces estrogen that causes her sexual nature and energy to express itself. A woman's sexual expression is reactive and accommodating. A woman's sexual energy causes her vagina to secrete during arousal. That secretion is designed to accept the penetration of a MAN'S erection allowing for a pleasurable exchange.

I do understand that oral and anal sex is also a form of penetration. But just let me keep things simple. I'm not a sex guru nor do I want to be so I will move on. Understand that I want you to also keep it simple. Just address the primary sexual tendencies of the masculine and feminine energies.

Men seek women and women respond sexually to men by design. So never ever try to stop the flow of nature. It's perfectly normal for you to have sexual desires.

The sex force in humans is biological and is driven by our sensory functions. That's why if a man is erect or if a woman gets wet, they will consider having sex with someone they barely know or care about. Sexual energy has nothing to do with the heart and soul. It's all physical in its rawest form.

I want you to keep it real with me. Have you ever had a one nightstand? Have you ever had sex with someone that you had little to nothing in common with? Have you ever just given in and slept with that dude who was "chasing" your booty because you were horny?

Sex is a physical act that is generated by sexual desires, in its basic operation. If you don't have a sexual desire, or if there is no testosterone or estrogen being generated, causing blood to flow and your body to respond sexually, then you "can't" have sex. It doesn't take love or romance to have sex. All it takes is a sexual desire.(Or some KY jelly)

Think about this. I can be in love with you, be romantically connected to you, and still not be able to have sex with you. If I can't get it up (erection), or if I don't desire to have sex, then we won't be able to get it on. (We can cuddle though)

Now on the flip side, I don't have to respect, like, or even desire a relationship with you and can still have sex (good sex of course), with you. As long as there is a desire and a natural body response (erection/secretion), we can get it on.

Sex "Myth"

What would you say is the biggest myth women believe about sex? I would say it's the, "if a man sleeps with me he must care about me" myth.

Like I stated earlier, things like care, respect, and love can have nothing to do with sex. Sex is a physical act. It can and in my opinion "should" be combined with the soul and heart's desire if it is to be special. However, the soul and spirit isn't needed to have sex. Although the soul and spirit are affected by sex; the soul and spirit's involvement isn't necessary for sexual intercourse to occur.

$1 Million Dollar Question

- Can a man "truly" be in love with me and sleep with another woman?

DivaGirl - How To Have A Good Man Find You

$100 Million Dollar Answer
- Of course he can.

It happens all of the time. People cheat on the people they love. I can feel you asking me, why they do what they do? Let me explain. Now follow along.

> I believe that women invest more **Emotional** attachment to the act of sex then men do (there are exceptions to the rule)
> I believe that men invest more **Logical** contemplation into the act of sex than women do.

- So what does that mean Rich?

I believe men and women take away two different levels of satisfaction from a sexual experience. I believe that men are more geared at satisfying a physical need (we want a nut), and to satisfy the ego (I'm the man).

I believe that women are more geared at satisfying an emotional need (he wants me) and a social one (we'll be together), during a sexual encounter. Now don't get me wrong. This is just a rule of thumb. It doesn't apply to every man and to every woman.

Principle #17 - Sex can involve the soul and spirit but it doesn't have to in order to take place.

I personally believe that men are more apt to separating love from sex, or sex from wanting a relationship; more than women tend to do. I believe it's easier for a man to think or say "this is just sex, nothing more nothing less" than it is for a woman to think and say. Remember babygirl, by design your feminine nature is nurturing and extremely emotionally receptive to the masculine nature.

I do believe that it's neither healthy, nor beneficial to

separate sex from romance and love. However, it is a fact that many of us *do* separate sex from romance and love. It is a fact that in this culture males are taught to separate sex from their emotions and heart. That's why, I believe men cheat to satisfy a sexual urge and the ego's standard. Meanwhile, I believe women cheat to satisfy an emotional one.

Now don't think I'm naïve. I know there are women that cheat to satisfy sexual urges, and there are men that cheat to satisfy emotional ones.

It's true, we are all sexual creatures. Therefore, don't be surprised or ashamed if you find yourself sexually attracted to other men, even though you're married or in a relationship already. For those of you that "try" to lie to yourself because you think being sexually attracted to someone else while in a relationship is "lust", you are fighting a losing battle.

It's all good and perfectly fine for you to be sexually attracted to other men. I would be a little concerned when you start to sexually desire other women.

Homosexuality & Bisexuality

*"They exchanged the truth of God for a lie and worshipped and served created things rather than the Creator- who is forever praised. Amen. Because of this God gave them over to shameful lusts. Even their women exchanged **natural** relations for unnatural ones. In the same way the men abandoned **natural** relations with women and were inflamed with lust for one another. Men committed indecent acts with other men and received in themselves the due penalty for their perversion."*
(Roman 1:26, 27 NIV)

Have you ever seen two female squirrels trying to get a nut… with each other? Have you ever seen two male dogs trying to get their "freak" on… *without a bitch*? I don't think so. To my understanding humans are the only creatures in nature that participate in unnatural sexual relations. What I mean by "unnatural", is in opposition of their primary sexual design and tendency. To my understanding, only humans have homosexual, bisexual, trisexual, quadsexual, or any other "unnatural" sexual relation that people engage in today.

Nature states that in order to have a complete sexual expression you need a masculine (assertive) principle and a feminine (accommodating) principle. By design those two principles work together to create a complete sexual expression, which also can reproduce. During every sexual encounter the masculine and feminine principles must exist. Someone has to give and someone has to receive.

Two men in their natural states aren't built to have a complete sexual expression or reproduce together. In their natural states, two men would represent two masculine (assertive) principles. That would make the sexual expression incomplete and reproduction impossible.

Two women in their natural states aren't built to have a sexual experience with each other. Two women in their natural states represent two feminine (accommodating) principles. That would make the sexual expression incomplete and reproduction impossible.

In order for two men (masculine principles) to engage in a homosexual encounter, their natural states have to be altered. In order for two women (feminine principles) to engage in a homosexual encounter, their natural states have to be altered as well. I used the above verse of scripture not to preach to anyone (ain't my MO), but to reveal a point.

Due to man's consciousness and our God like mental capabilities, we can make decisions against the flow of nature. Remember, we have the knowledge of both good and evil (read Genesis). Therefore, I believe that man is the only creature that has this ability to alter and pervert his sexuality.

Animals don't possess the mental capacities of humans. Animals instinctively obey their design and nature. That explains why we don't see cats barking like dogs or see two female cats licking each other down..

Men and women have been given the creative ability of God. Therefore, we can "create", or act outside of our God design and nature.

A man can "playfully" act like a woman. A woman can "playfully" act like a man. Actors make a living and career for themselves by altering their states and natures. So it's something we *can* do as humans. However, a man can never truly "become" a woman and a woman can never truly "become" a man. Despite, what modern technology and surgical procedure may indicate, a man will never become a woman, and vise versa.

Now let me ask you a question. If a man and woman can "playfully" pervert or alter their design and natural tendency for fun. Do you think it's possible for people to do so sexually? Of course we can. It happens all day everyday. Men sexually take on the accommodating (feminine principle) nature of a woman, and sleep with other men. Women sexually take on the assertive (masculine principle) nature of a man and have sex with other women.

Remember, you always need a masculine (assertive) principle and a feminine (accommodating) principle to have sexual intercourse. That's why the natural states must be perverted and altered for a homosexual encounter to occur.

I can just hear and see all of the gay/lesbian rights activist coming at me, with the picket signs, hate mail, and nonsense. I guess that's why so many preachers and pastors have stayed away from the subject (Bad press). I'm here to say it loud and clear for all to hear. Homosexual encounters are *unnatural.* A man with a man or a woman with a woman sexually goes against the natural sexual force and flow of harmony.

* So what are you saying Rich, are homosexuals and bisexuals wrong for what they do? You know people are born that way.

I'm not here making right or wrong calls. I just wanted to make a point. If you think people are born that way, I need for you to show me a female baby born that wants to sleep with another female baby. Show me a male baby trying to holla at another male baby sexually in the nursery. Once again, I'm not trying to be facetious. I just want someone to bring that to my attention. If you find that going on let me know ASAP.

To my understanding, sexuality is learned through experience, exploration, and association. So get back at me if I'm wrong (I'm open minded). I never said I knew it all. I'm always willing to learn.

This book isn't about homosexual or bisexual activities. So if you have any questions, comments, or information that you want to share with me, email it or write me. I'm always willing to have a civilized conversation and learn new things, so hit me up.

For the books sake, I will sum it up like this. There is a sexual force in the world that vibrates in men and women alike. Men, primarily possess the masculine sexual nature and women primarily, possess the feminine sexual nature. When in their natural state, men will sexually desire women and women will sexually desire men.

In an unnatural state, a man can sexually desire another man and a woman can sexually desire another woman. Humans have the ability to pervert and alter their natural states by choice. As a result, it's only in human relations that you will witness a homosexual or bisexual act.

So for all of you sexy bisexual women reading this book, understand that although many men may find two women "gettin' it on" a beautiful thing, you're still going against the grain, luv.

Let Me Romance Ya

What's your concept of romance? When you think of a "romantic" evening what crosses your mind? Is it candles, soft music, rose pedals, a black sand beach, a good smelling man?

121

Think about it. In fact, right it down and be as descriptive as you can be with it.

Now that you've finished with that. You know I have something extra for you. Would you be mad at me if I said romance isn't what you've been taught and lead to believe?

All of those romance novels, soap operas, or other "romantic" inspired material you've allowed into your system are limited and incomplete.

Romance is not what "they" say it is (Here we go again). Romance is a force too many of us know nothing about. In fact, what the average person calls "love", is actually "romance". So let me ask you, how do you know when you are "in love". I'll bet a thousand dollars that what you're calling "love", is *romance*.

$1 Million Dollar Question

■ How can you say what I call "love" is romance. You don't know me Rich?

$10 Million Dollar Answer

■ Unless you're still "in love" with that person and not only "have love" for them, what you called "love" was *romance*.

There are only a small percentage of us that actually know what romance is. The majority of us only identify with sex and love. So when there's a force greater than sex manifesting in the relationship, we call it "love". Just because we are currently doing something, or just because something is all we know, doesn't mean it's "right". We've been conditioned to see only sex and love. Romance is for the chosen. Many of us don't see romance.

Do me a favor, think about the most romantic movie you have ever saw. Think about your favorite romantic scene, got it. Now, I'm sorry babygirl but I have to rain on your parade once more. I have to "hate" for a little bit. (Please forgive me)

Chances are even your favorite romantic movie and your favorite "romantic" scene isn't romance at all. Now I really have your wheels turning right? I can just hear you saying, "So what in the hell is "romance"? Be easy divagirl (That's your new pet name). I'll answer that for you. Better yet, I'll let you answer that for yourself, first.

I think that's a better idea anyway because all of your life's answers are within you anyhow. So in my usual style, I'll ask you some questions (I love a smart sexy woman). All you have to do is answer them.

<u>Romance IQ</u>

* When do you feel more connected to your man?
A). When you snoop around through his things and make discoveries about him for the first time.
B). When you have an honest and open-minded conversation with him about whatever pops up.

* What do you prefer?
A). To keep your aspirations and plans all to yourself.
B). To share your aspirations and plans with a supportive mate that encourages your efforts.

* What feels better to you?
A). A slap on the ass with a " Damn you got a phat ass".
B). A warm secure embrace, a soft kiss, with a "I've missed you so much today baby tell me all about your day."

* What's more exciting for you?
A). Already knowing what your man is gonna say before he opens his mouth.
B). Getting to know your man and new interesting things about him.

Okay, are you finished answering the questions? If you answered (B) to all of the questions then you know what romance truly is. See I told you, you would know.

Romance is when the souls of two people opens up and vibrates on the same frequency together. Romance is the force that connects your personality to someone else's (we have so much in common). Romance is the force that connects your goals and aspirations to another person's (We want the same things out of life). Romance is the time when your feelings, desires, and dominant thoughts connects with another person's.

Think of it like this: Remember when you thought you were "falling in love". That time when you and Mr. Lover were getting to know so many interesting things about each other? That time when y'all used to kiss, hug, and look into each other's souls? You know what I'm talking about divagirl. That time when it was "all good in da hood". That time when everyday was a "good day". Remember when you were skipping to work, whistling in the morning, and telling your girls all about him.

I understand why anyone would call that force "love", but that was *romance*. Only after examining the situation will we realize that it wasn't love after all. That force could not be love. And here's why.

* God is love and God is unchanging
God is the same yesterday, today, and will be tomorrow.

Therefore love is unchanging. Love is the same yesterday, today, and will be the same tomorrow.

So what are you saying Rich? I'm saying, it's impossible to "fall in and out of love". What we call "falling in and out of love", is finding and losing the romantic vibe of a relationship.

Romance is of the soul. Love is of the spirit. As a result, love is unchanging divagirl. When you love someone, you will always love that person. However, romance can come and go in and out of the relationship. Remember romance is when the soul openly vibrates with another person's soul.

If you and your mate start lying, stop communicating, and stop learning new things about one another, the romance will fade

(You'll stop "vibing"). If you two stop the affectionate interacting the romance will diminish eventually.

When couples stop speaking honestly, when couples stop communicating, stop hugging, holding, kissing, the sexual intensity will also wane. The sex may still be good physically, meaning both individual's climax. However, the soul satisfaction won't be there anymore.

I'm quite sure you know what I'm talking about. Remember what the sex felt like when you were "in love" with Mr. Casanova. Not only would your body explode but your soul felt good too, didn't it. Now think about what the sex felt like when you weren't "in love" anymore. Didn't it feel like something was missing? You probably thought you weren't "making love" anymore, right baby?

The truth is if you and Mr. Casanova were "truly" in love, then the love was still there. It was the "romance" that left the equation. Think about it, even the sex was the same. He still had the same equipment and you still had the same spot, right?

$1 Million Dollar Question

■ So all of those times I thought I was "falling in and out of love" were bogus?

$10 Million Dollar Answer

■ Absolutely baby. You never "fall in love". Therefore if you never "fall in", you will never "fall out" of it.

Do you now understand a little bit more the force of romance? Romance is the key and body of the relationship. Rarely do you spiritually connect with someone and "find love". It's the romance that we commonly associate with in our relationships. Since so many of us think that "love" is "romance", we also believe that we can "love" today and "hate" tomorrow. In truth, few of us operate in "love". Yet, it's a phrase we throw around like a ping ball.

It's romance and sex that we normally deal with. It's the

body and soul that we communicate with the most within our human dealings.

The Romanticless Society

Our culture today doesn't promote love and romance like it used to. Today, it's all about ass, titts, cars, rims, meaningless sex, and game playing. The "urban" community has traded in love for money, bling bling, and superficial encounters. The music industry, movie industry, and the mass media are all promoting and profiting off of sex, violence, and the destruction of our souls. We have really forfeited our souls for a few punk ass dollars.

There are more court shows and scandalous talk shows on television than family programs and cartoons. But then again, today's cartoons are worst than the damn talk shows. And who knows what a family is anymore? There is more lust, violence, and disrespect in our music than love, romance, and respect. We are becoming more and more desensitized by the minute.

One of the reasons why I use the language that I do, when I write is because you might not hear me if I didn't.

If we shut down emotionally and become too hard and cold, how are we supposed to lovingly interact with one another? Without a loving interaction, how are we to build families and prosper as a community? If all we do is dog one another out, how are we to openly communicate? If men and women aren't getting along, then what will happen to our world? Remember, it all began with one God, one man, and one woman. Don't kill the romance.

It's no surprise to me that if you want a chart topping song, book, or movie all you have to do is display disrespect and exploits the sexual desires of people.

It's no surprise to me when I hear eleven year old boys calling little girls "bitches", "chickenheads", "birds", and "ho's". It's no surprise to me that kids are losing their virginity and innocence earlier and earlier.

Every generation is to be more advanced and effective than

the last. My concern are the things our children are now more advanced and effective in than we were. Little girls are having babies and raising families as single mothers', right after they take off their training bra. Little boys are thinking they're the man of the house because he supports his mother and sisters with his dirty drug money. What the f#&K is going on out here? What are we doing? Where are we going?

We have stopped singing, writing, and aspiring to love and romance each other as men and women. It's now about manipulating, "game playing", and abusing. We're not really making the effort to get to know each other anymore. We don't want to take long walks, picnic in the park, or sit by the fireplace and just talk.

We don't want to explore each other's souls anymore. All we want to know now is how much money you have, how big is the dick, how fat is the ass, or how good is the head/sex.

All we want to know is how we're gonna get what we want from the other person.

When we meet in the club, on the corner, on campus, or in the church, it's not because we are really interested in each other.

We've stopped courting, asking each other meaningful questions, and listening for answers. We rush into every sunny day and run away from the rainy days.

We would rather bump and grind than slow dance. We would rather argue, than pray with each other. We would rather complain about what someone is not doing for us, rather than compliment them for what they are doing. We would rather watch "How High" than "Love Jones". We would rather listen to Scarface than Babyface.

I would like to think that this problem was only a "man thing", but you women have now caught up. I'm always amazed in the club at how wild women get when a Little Kim song comes on. I never know if I should continue to dance with the female, or get a hotel room. The romance is gone.

I believe that we have to be more conscious and monitor

our intake more than ever before. If you listen to rap music, watch soap operas, Ricki Lake, and divorce court all day long. If you are always reading the newspaper, always watching the news, and surround yourself with bitter and pessimistic people, don't be surprised if you stop trusting people. Don't be surprised if you stop believing in love.

Understand divagirl that our culture and society promotes ignorance, fear, hate, and division. Think about this. With all of the information available today, with all of the cable channels to choose from: Why is it that you are hearing many of the things in this book for the first time? The romance is gone.

Do you think that chivalry and romance is dead? Do you think men have stopped being gentlemen? Do you think men would rather just have sex, than to build a satisfying relationship? Now I have a better question for you to answer.

Do you think men today **KNOW** how to be gentlemen and make a relationship work? Do you think males are being trained and taught to be gentlemen, husbands, and fathers? I don't think so.

Listen to and look at the messages this romanticless society is telling our males. Listen to the rap music, watch the videos, and take notice of how manhood is now portrayed on television.

A lot of males become "niggers" and "suckers" because that's all they know. Trust me on that.

Contrary to public assumption, men want romance and love too. Men also possess a soul and spirit (I know many don't show it). Our culture doesn't teach courtship or teach us what "romance" and "love" is. We think sex is a "who's dick is bigger, who's ass is fatter, let's try to get a nut" game men and women play. The romance is gone.

Whatever happened to that innocent boyish and girlish crush? Whatever happened to that "let's really take our time to get to know each other" phase? What happened to the "I think you are special, so let's wait awhile" mentality? The romance is gone.

We cannot produce quality by rushing its completion. We

cannot produce a scared entity, with quantity (I hit that too). If you want something special then put special qualities into the equation.

Romance is precious and "shouldn't" be taken lightly. Romance isn't love, but it's the closet thing next to it. It's impossible to sustain a romantic connection with a person over a period of time, and not "find" love with that person.

Unfortunately, we left romance, chivalry, and love for the old folk. Too bad we traded in that deep conversation for a quickie. Too bad we stopped believing in love and respecting the dynamics between men and women. Too bad we let the love and romance between us go baby. I really miss what we had. It was special. It was precious. Now look at us. All we have is lust, disrespect, and mistrust. The romance is gone.

That Four Letter Word

So far we've talked about sex and romance. We've discussed the principles and difference between sex and romance. But we haven't discussed the principles and power of love. If sex ain't love and romance ain't love, then what is "love"?

Love is one hundred percent more than you currently think. Love is the supreme energy and force. It's because of love that the world exists. Love is the creative force in all living things. Love is infinite. From a metaphysical standpoint, love is the ultimate connector. God is love.

Trust me I know that this all sounds good. I know you're probably wondering, what does all of this mean in practical terms? In practical terms, love is the ultimate meaning behind all things of substance. Love is why you mother your children. Love is why you have family and friends. Love is why people pursue their dreams and passions. Love is why you would help that homeless or hungry person on the street. Love is why you volunteer your resources to help a cause. Love is why that man and that woman are together for the long haul. Love is why we live.

When love dies, so shall our world end. When you cease to

a have a loving cause in your life, people to love, and when you stop receiving love from others, you are as good as dead. We need to give and receive love in life in order to have meaning, significance, and satisfaction. It's true: Love is all we need.

"I Hate You!"

Right now we are living in the best and worst of times. African Americans in particular are experiencing great highs on some levels but experiencing devastating lows on many others.

We have more access to more opportunities and possess more material wealth than ever before. Yet, despite all of that our families, communities, and intimate relationships are breaking down. Black men and black women are not getting along. Black men are tired of the "Black woman's attitude" and Black women are tired of the "Black man's struggle". As a result, even in the midst of prosperous times, people are angry, lonely, and hopeless.

Despite all of the gains that have been made people are still "hatin`". I want to address the "hatin`" that is going on between the man and the woman today.

What year was it when love and respect went out of style? Why is it cool and fashionable for a man to hate a woman? When did it become sporty for women to be so disrespectful and angry towards men? Did we forget how this whole game got started? Don't we realize we are destroying ourselves? Don't we know when men and women stop loving each other that's when this party ends?

Divagirl, are you "hating" men right now? Do you "hate" your father for not being there? Do you "hate" your ex husband or ex boyfriend for cheating on you? Do you "hate" the asshole that fondled and molested you as a little girl? Do you "hate" Black men for not being there for you during slavery, childbirth and at nights to hold you close? Do you hate some man right now at this very moment?

Let It Go

If there is some man or if there are several men you are "hatin'"... let it go. Hate hinders progress and cuts you off from your reserved blessings. So if you believe deep down that happiness, satisfaction, and prosperity is yours let the hate go.

If you believe that there is some man around the corner, that is "right" for you, let the hate go so he'll find you. Whatever it is that you are asking for is being put on hold right now. Not because you don't deserve to have it. Whatever it is that you really want is being put on hold because of the hate you're holding onto.

My acronym for hate, is Having Angered To Extreme (HATE). Some man caused you pain and it hurt you. You nurtured that hurt to the point of anger. Once you became angry, you mixed it with some negative thinking and unforgiveness. Once that combination matured you manifested hate. So you went all the way from a frustrating, disappointing, or painful experience into a state of hate. Now I need you to do yourself and the world a favor. Let the hate go.

Take three deep breaths and calmly let it go divagirl. It's time to let forgiveness be a blessing in your life. Forgive your father, he was wrong. Forgive your baby father, he is immature. Forgive your husband, he is ignorant and makes poor decisions. Let forgiveness purge your system right now.

There is no sense in walking around another day with "hate" in your system when it's "love" that you want. Let the hate go, forgive them, forgive him, forgive yourself.

If you have to write a letter accepting your father's forgiveness. Reach out to those men that have caused you great pain in the past.

You have to let go of the hate, if you are to experience love in you life and relationships. If you "hate" men, how can they "love" you in return? Remember you give to receive babygirl. There are too many blessings awaiting you for you to allow the "hate" to hold you back.

That promotion awaits you. That relationship with Mr. "right" is calling. That peace of mind, fulfillment, and success you dreamed about, is knocking. So let the hate go and lovingly open up. I promise, you'll never be the same because of it.

<u>**Love Is Love**</u>

"Love is patient, love is kind. It does not envy, it does not boast, it is not proud. It is not rude, it is not self seeking, it is not easily angered, it keeps no records of wrongs. Love does not delight in evil but rejoices with the truth. It always protects, always trusts, always hopes, always preserves. Love never fails"
(1Corinthians 13:4-8 NIV)

I briefly talked about forgiveness and letting the "hate" go, because that is how love lives. Love can only be compared to love because it's incomparable. Love is indescribable. Words limit and restrict, and love is infinite.

Love isn't something that we think. It's something that we know. God is love and God is truth. Therefore, love is true and impossible to find through fear, manipulation, and deceit. Why do you think I bring that up? I bring it up because you cannot manipulate or trick a man into loving you. You cannot plot or force your way to love. The only way to love is through truth and life.

Love exists in the "real world". You don't have to die or go to "heaven" to find it. Love is truth. You don't have to lie or pretend to be something in order to have it. Love flows. You don't have to work hard to find it.

After you have released the hate, fear, and manipulating schemes from out of your system, you are on your way to finding love. Once you accept yourself as good and Godly, while seeing those same qualities in everyone else, you will find love. I know that many of you ladies have been told false things about love. So here are five truths about love:

DivaGirl - How To Have A Good Man Find You

Five Truths of Love

1. Love doesn't hurt it heals
2. You never "fall" in love, you "find" love
3. Love is eternal, it always exist and remains the same
4. Love loves even when you don't want to love
5. Love is of the spirit it's greater than emotions

"Finding" Love

Let's keep in line with one of the reasons why you paid fifteen dollars for this book. You want a loving relationship with that special man, right? You want a relationship that will naturally lead to marriage, right? So if that is the case then understand this. You and Mr. Man have to 'find" love together.

*   What does "finding love" mean Rich?

Thanks for asking. Now let me answer that for you sweetheart. Within all of us there is a point of truth, a center where we really exist. Behind the make up, weave, body, personality, career, religious affiliation, behind all of that there is your connection to God.

It's at your core, your essence of being, where love dwells. Your core and essence isn't all wrapped up into the world like your ego may be. Your essence doesn't care about age, race, height, weight, or any of that other stuff we make important when selecting a mate. Your core is free and without judgment. All it does is "know" and "love".

To find love with a person you have to connect to their core and center. You have to meet the spirit, the "real" person.

On the surface that might sound very deep but it's not that serious. The truth is "finding" love is the easiest thing for us to do, once we kill the ego and then give up trying to satisfy false beliefs.

It's our ego, fears, and petty judgments that prevent us from "finding" love. Once you are comfortable enough within yourself, to be yourself, you'll "find" love for yourself. Once you open up and allow people to be themselves, you'll "find" love with other people.

Once you give up telling people who they "should" be, you'll "find" love with who they are. Once you release your pains and fears of men allowing them to express their compliment to your womanhood, you'll "find" love with a man.

Once you sincerely walk through life, men will naturally respond to you in a loving way. When you are loving you vibrate at a greater frequency and radiate with good spirits. Men will magnetically be attracted to you. They will see love in your demeanor, in your smile, hear it in your words, and feel it in your presence.

Let me tell you a little secret. Men are craving love more than anything else today. Trust me, men really desire love, more than just some ass. The loving woman today will have far more long term success with men than the "beauty queen" or "stripper". I know for some of you it may be hard to believe that in the long run it's going to be your spirit and inside that wins Mr. "right" over, but it is. Trust me, it will be your spirit that Mr. "right" loves.

Principle #18- Your body can get you a night, but your spirit gets you a lifetime.

Don't ever underestimate the power of love. Don't ever take for granted the essence of who you are. You will find love with "Mr. right" after the initial "I'm trying to impress you" stage wears off.

When you introduce the "real" you and not only your physical beauty, titles, or "things" to that man, you'll find love. Keep in mind, what you give will be multiplied and given back to you. So the key to "finding" love with Mr. Right is to be loving.

To find love all you have to do is be the beautiful woman that dwells in your essence. Leave the ego and hate in the world for those that are miserable. I'm telling you a beautiful woman on the inside and outside is irresistible to a man.

Remember, once you fully embrace your womanhood, your compliment and partner in life, is a "man". The "boys", "sons", "pimps", and the "dogs" that don't know what love is won't connect long term or very deeply with you.

So be a loving woman and watch a loving man walk into your life. To "find" love with Mr. "right", you have to introduce him to your core. You have to meet his core openly. Love is for the pure. Love is spiritual. Can you handle it baby?

Conclusion

I know this chapter was the longest so far and we covered a lot within it. I hope that I have helped to make things a little bit clearer for you. Hopefully you now understand the difference between sex, romance, and love. Hopefully, you now understand and appreciate the force of all three.

Remember they are all different energies that work to make a relationship holistic, fulfilling, and meaningful. Just in case you forgot some of what we covered here are the chapter's key points.

Key Points to Remember

* Sex is a physical act. Sex can be performed with or without love and romance. To have meaningful sex and to satisfy the soul, romance is needed. To "make love" the spirit, soul, and body must all be involved.

* Romance is of the soul. It's connecting with the emotions, desires, and dominant thoughts of another person. Romance is the body of the relationship. As long as a couple is being affectionate, honestly communicating, supporting each other, learning, and exploring each other's soul, then the romance will live on. Romance can come and go in and out of a relationship. The good news is, if it goes, a couple can always get it back.

* Love is spirit. To "find" love with someone you have to

connect with their essence and the God within them. Love is truth and life. It can only be revealed to a couple as they connect to "who they are" and not "who they want to be". Love is eternal. It always remains the same. Therefore, once you "find" love with someone, you'll never "lose" it. Even if your mind and body doesn't know where the love has gone, your spirit will know. Love supercedes sex and romance.

* Your physical beauty (looks, body, walk, etc) are all sex stimulators. Your personality, plans, preferences, goals, and conversation, are all soul connectors. Your spirit and essence, is the love in you.

In closing realize that you have much more to offer a man than sex. So how big your ass is, or how pretty your face may be, shouldn't be your only focus. Your soul and spirit are the "quality" in you, so don't compromise it. Nurture and offer your soul. Let your spirit shine bright, along with that pretty face and lovely body. I guarantee you men will come running. Men want women.

A beautiful woman on the inside and out is a rare find and precious jewel these days. So be that rare commodity and watch your stock rise through the roof. Well whatever it is that you do, always remember that sex ain't love.

FYI

If you haven't already, go out to your local bookstore and pick up my other books Punaney Galore and Real Men Do Real Things. They are stories that deal with all of these issues and much, much, much…more.

OR

Log onto: **richpublications.com** to order

CHAPTER 7

It's All Hype: Why "D-Low Brothers" Really Ain't Your Problem

"I cashed in my retirement plan, told my boss where he could stick it, bought $120,000.00 worth of can goods with my retirement monies, changed my religious beliefs, locked myself in the basement...and nothing happened. I did all of that and it was all just a bunch of hype. Now I'm without any savings, unemployed, can't stand the site of a canned good, praying to a new God...and I'm still locked in my basement."

Ms. Dumdum Dilly due to the Y2K phenomenon

INTRODUCTION

What's more sensational than fear? What moves people to talking and doing the ridiculous more than a good *"you're about to die/the world is coming to an end"* type of message?
Exactly...*nothing*

At this present time nothing has you women more shocked than this whole "he's living on the D-Low" phenomenon, which has swept through this country like a wicked witch on a broom. I can barely watch television with my wife before her homophobic ass will attempt to persuade me that some dude on the tube is a "lollipop" (meaning gay or bisexual). I mean literally everyday she is pointing out someone new who she believes is on the "down

137

low". But what's even worst than my wife, are the countless times women have said to my partner Tom as he is selling our book, "Real Men do Real Things..."*is this one of those down low type of books?"*

Can you believe that here a man is showing a female a book entitled **"Real Men Do Real Things"**, and the first thing that pops out of her mouth is, *"is this one of those down low type of books?"* (And she says it with a snotty attitude)

Now my next question to you is this...*WHAT THE F#&K IS GOING ON, ladies?* I know at this point you realize just how sensitive I am to the images and associations we make today when referring to men. And there is nothing that is more upsetting to me than this whole "Down Low" bullshit (excuse the French). It's so bad today that many women and this might include you: You all think that the reason why you're not in a healthy relationship with a man is because..."they are living on the D-Low".

NEWSFLASH: THE D-LOW BROTHER REALLY AIN'T
YOUR PROBLEM BOOBOO.

And of course I'll take the time to explain.

Ray Charles Could See That!

Did you see the movie Ray? (If you didn't you need to go check that out because Jamie Fox did his thing) But even if you didn't see the movie, I'll share with you what I thought was the most profound element of the movie. I was amazed to find out just how much Ray Charles could "see" as a blind man. The man actually used his hands, ears, and more importantly his mind to navigate himself through life with an amazing degree of self-sufficiency. Ray Charles was so self-sufficient that he was able to live by himself...I said live by himself. The man who "couldn't see" was able to live alone. Now I don't know about you but that was crazy to me. Here we have a blind man living alone while my cousin Bobby can't seem to get his seeing ass up off of my aunts couch and into his own place (That's a jokey joke).

Seriously speaking though, I feel that many of you women pretend to be deaf, dumb, and blind when dealing with men today. I find it extremely hard to believe that you women today don't see a gay man when you're looking at him. I find it highly difficult to accept that you ladies today don't feel a gay man when you're in the presence of one. I mean come on Booboo let's keep it real, since when did it become so hard to spot a man that was a little light in the ass? I don't care if a man plays professional football for the Dallas Cowboys or preaches on Sunday morning to a twenty thousand member congregation, how could you not see, feel, or hear "something" that would warrant, "something?"

Wisdom Gem* Denial is the worst form of self-pity that exist.

. I believe many of you women deny what you see, hear, and feel when dealing with a bisexual, or "D-Low Brother" because....**YOU WANT A MAN.** And to be honest with you there is nothing wrong with a woman wanting a man. In fact it's perfectly healthy and natural. But I just have this to say:

If you want "a man" in your life, then you are gonna have to deal with "a man" in life in order to truly be satisfied.

The reason why I don't think the "D-Low Brother" is the problem like many of you are lead to believe, is because of this:

Too many women haven't seen a man around in a long while.

Due to the fatherlessness epidemic that I touched on earlier, many of you ladies grew up without the proper relationship to manhood. I mean you didn't grow up with the proper exposure to the compliment sex. Therefore, any and everything that shows up

<u>male</u> in your latter years of life you give credence to as being a **man**. And just in case you didn't know or simply forgot, I'll remind you: *A homosexual or bisexual <u>male</u> is not the same as a heterosexual **man**, and it's not hard to decipher between them.*

Many of you haven't been exposed to the "ways" of a man in a while. You have forgotten what we sound like, how we walk, what we make you feel like in our presence. It's sad but many of you ladies only consistent exposure to the compliment sex is your son, whom you're growing to become a feminized male, the brother or uncle that calls and writes from jail every so often, or the males you see in your church, many of whom in my opinion are the biggest homosexuals and bisexuals in the game. And all of this is affecting your vision.

PRINCIPLE #19 - There are two types of people that can't see: Those who are blind and those in denial.

Check This Out:

Let's say that you walk into your favorite restaurant and are as hungry as a hostage. You sit down at the table and tell the waiter, "Bring me out something to eat." Upon hearing your request the waiter goes back into the kitchen and brings you out a nice hot plate of dog food with a ice-cold manure shake. Now remember, all you said to the waiter was, "Bring me out something to eat", and that's exactly what he did. He brought you out "something" to eat?

Now let's say you walk into that same restaurant, with the same hunger, and tell that same waiter, "Can I have a steak cooked medium well?" What would happen if the waiter came back to your table with a bowl of chilly? You would obviously tell him, "Oh that's not what I ordered, you must have the wrong table", right? See once you clearly recognize a thing, it's easy to decipher between "what is" and "what's not".

If you're asking for a " heterosexual **man**" to step into your world and for some reason a "homosexual/bisexual" <u>male</u> walks up to your table, how difficult will it be for you to see… "Oh that's not what I ordered, you must have the wrong table", once you know what a heterosexual man looks like? As a woman, once you come to grips with what a **man** is, the homosexual or "D-Low brother" is no longer an issue for you. If you can identify what a man is, it's easy to see what is not (Get it).

No More Funny Business

Now is the time that we really cut the games and get down to the real. Ladies, ladies, my precious ladies, I have a life saving piece of advice for you all. And it's this:

IF YOU EVER HAVE TO QUESTION A MALE'S SEXUALITY THAT IS A CLEAR INDICATION THAT HE ISN'T THE MAN YOU'RE LOOKING FOR…PERIOD

A heterosexual man is **100% HETEROSEXUAL**, he's thorough all the way through. Meaning you're not sticking anything in his ass, he ain't wearing your clothes, he ain't gonna feel soft and pink to you, he's not gonna switch when he walks, or sings when he talks (You know what I'm talkin' about). A heterosexual **man** is 100% heterosexual without error, meanwhile a bisexual male is 50/50, and the homosexual male is 0%. See, even the bisexual, or "D-Low" chump will expose his 50% gay side to you, *if you pay attention*. And when he does expose himself with his "non-heterosexual" behavior, you know what that means…**IT'S TIME TO GO!** When a male shows you some "funny business", it's time to reconsider everything that was up until that point.

Sexual Mathematics

Heterosexual Man	= 100% Heterosexual characteristics
Bi-Sexual Male	= 50% Heterosexual characteristics
Homosexual Male	= 0% Heterosexual characteristics

PRINCIPLE #20 - It's impossible for a child to not look like both its mother and its father, for the child is made up of them both. It's also impossible for a bi-sexual male to not display both sides of his sexuality, for his sexuality is made up of both heterosexual and homosexual characteristics.

When you look in the mirror don't you see both your mother and father's features? Look at your son or daughter, doesn't he/she look like both you and their father? Exactly, that's why I'm not buying the whole "I didn't know he was gay" sob story that women cry when they "discover" their man of five years was a pillow biter… "on the low". Open up your eyes ladies and put an end to all of this funny business that we have going on. **MEN ARE 100% HETERSOSEXUAL**…got that! So if you happen to see my man Tom on the street selling "Real Men Do Real Things", I'm gonna lose my cool if I find out you asked him that question… *"Is this one of those down low type of books?"*

What's The Problem Now?

Now based on all that we just covered, do you still think the "D-Low Brother" is your problem? I was amazed to find out just how many of you women either bought or read that "On The Down Low" book that was recently featured on the Ophray Winfrey Show. My rationale is this; why do you need to know what a homosexual or bisexual *male's* tendencies are when you're looking for a heterosexual **man** anyway? To me that's ass backwards. My logic is this: if you want a man in your life then you need to **rediscover what a man is** and **what you really want from one** (but that's just me). I'm figuring why would I go to school and study law, if I wanted to become a heart surgeon? I'm just curious as to why you ladies are so interested in homosexual and bisexual men? I just don't get that one.

See I think too many of us are focusing on <u>sensation</u> and "<u>bullshit</u>"… and it's killing us.

It's sensational for you to think and talk about the whole "D-Low" dynamic. You're like *"Wow he's sleeping with a man...and he's married with children...Girl please"* You're fascinated by it all and yet fearful thinking, *"Girl you have to be careful out here today because all of these niggas are into God knows what."* It's sad but many of you ladies believe that there are more homosexual and bisexual <u>males</u> out in the world today than there are heterosexual **men**. (Especially my African American sisters) And to me that's **150% BULLSHIT!**

It's this sensationalized "D-Low" mentality that is killing the fabric of you ladies expectations when dealing with men today. Never before has there been so much fear of the bi-sexual man...and he has been around for ages (Just ask your grandmother). Homosexual and bisexual <u>males</u> are not a new discovery in society. But then again anything that is dramatized also becomes sensationalized, so I guess that's the reason why bisexual ("D-Low") males seem larger than life nowadays.

Wisdom Gem* Everything increases in size and appearance once it's magnified. You can take the thinnest string of hair and under the right magnification make it appear as large as O.J. Simpson's cranium.

I'm here to tell you: There are not more homosexual or bisexual <u>males</u> in the world today than there are heterosexual **men**. So your real problem isn't the "D-Low Brother". Your real issue is your lack of understanding regarding manhood and what being a man is all about. You have forgotten what a man is, you have forgotten how a man moves, and you have forgotten how a man talks. Now since this is the case, you definitely have to read the remaining chapters in this book and find out...How Men Really Get Down. I mean enough with the gay and "D-Low Brother" shenanigans already. It's time for you to rediscover what the heterosexual man is all about.

If you think about it, why is it so hard today for you women to spot a gay or bisexual <u>male</u>, especially since so many of them are openly flamboyant? But like I said, you first need to re-establish in your mind and soul what a man really is all about. You need to rediscover what a man's tendencies are, what a man likes, what a man wants, why men do what men do, etc...

Once you come to grips again with what a man is the "D-Low" brother will stick out like a sore thumb, no matter if he's your favorite rapper or your tough talkin`/gun toting boyfriend of six years. You will be able to clearly see a lollipop (bisexual man) when you see one. TRUST ME!

So meet me on the next page and I will expose you to the inner workings of the **HETEROSEXUAL MAN**. Remember it is him that you want anyway, right?

CHAPTER 8

"IS THAT IT?": WHAT MEN REALLY REALLY WANT

"SM seeking a SF ages 21-65yrs old. She can be short, tall, black, white, and everything in between. She can have a thin, petite, voluptuous, or large overweight body frame, she only has to be comfortable with herself, as she is. She can be a college graduate, a student, or a high school dropout, I only ask that her mind be right. She can be a Christian, Catholic, Muslim, or Buddhist, as long as she believes in more than just herself. She can have children or be childless. I just don't want any babyfather drama. She can be anything she wants to be. I only ask that she be all female. She must be all woman"

Single man's personal ad

INTRODUCTION

What do you think men really want? I often hear comedians making jokes about what men really want. They say, "that a man wants some head, his stomach fed, and silence." It may sound shallow and simple, but it's true. A man wants sex, a good meal, and silence, but then again so do you women.

That's why I won't talk about that which is obvious. I won't talk about what you may have already heard before. I'm going deep. I will share with you Ms. Lady the things men are

A beautiful woman on the inside and out is a rare find and precious jewel these days. So be that rare commodity and watch your stock rise through the roof. Well, whatever it is that you do, always remember that sex ain't love.
really searching for. I'm going to tell you what men really want. If you thought the book was good up until this point, it's about to get real good now.

Remember babygirl if you find this book to be helpful buy two more copies and bless your girls with their own. Never ever lend this book out, it's my gift to you. (Okay my luv)

The Men From The Boys

Before we get into this, I need to set the records straight. I need to make it clear whom we are about to talk about in this chapter.

This chapter is about what **men** really want. Remember there is a difference between a boy and a man. If you're accustomed to dealing with boys, this chapter might be a little too heavy for you to handle. You may be too young for this babygirl. If you are too young, I won't hold it against you so read along anyhow. I have to warn you though, this is for my grown and sexy folk.

A man and a boy's desires are as different as having a dollar to spend or having a million dollars to spend in the mall. Although they are both sums of money you will get far more "stuff" with a million dollars than you would with a dollar.

A man is on a completely different level than a boy. A man is more developed emotionally, he processes life from a greater consciousness, and his actions are mightier than that of a boy's. So understand, I will only talk about what men want.

As a beautiful (holistic) woman, it's men that you want to deal with and not "boys", anyhow. So I will coach you and help you out. I'm going to share with you what's really going on inside of the heart, soul, and body of a man.

DivaGirl - How To Have A Good Man Find You

I understand that you're used to getting your advice about men from women. My question is, how long have those women that you get your advice from been men? How long has mama and dem` been walking around in these male bodies and dealing with life as men? I thought so.

I know that some of them may be able to give you good advice. I understand that they may all be good intentioned. But not one of the women you get advice from is a man.

Therefore, all of their advice is from a female's perspective. So let me break it down for you and give you what those other women don't have the capacity to do. Let me (a man), tell you what men really want. I know that your gay hairdresser Raul has been trying to give you the male psyche in the salon for years. But he even thinks like a woman and deals with men from a feminine perspective.

So let me talk the talk babygirl. For those of you who are interested in learning about what "dogs", "boys", or "pimps" want, skip this chapter. This is for women only. I say this is for women only.

Something Ain't Right

"Then the Lord God took the man and put him in the Garden of Eden to work it...The Lord God said, "It is not good for the man to be alone. I will make a suitable helper for him...Then the Lord God made a woman from the rib he had taken out of the man...The man and his wife were both naked and they felt no shame"

(Genesis 2:16, 18, 22, 25 NIV)

At creation God hooked Adam (man) up. God gave man a winning formula for his fulfillment and success in life. God gave him all that he was designed to have in order to prosper as a man. If you didn't know, let me bring you on in. Adam was the man before his "fall". Adam was all of that and a bag of chips.

Adam was the prototype of manhood and success as a man. Like Jay Z, Adam had the blueprint. Ever since Adam's "fall" in the Garden of Eden man has been relentlessly looking for that formula for manhood and success again. I know you're thinking. So what's the formula?

At creation Adam (man) had three things that set the tone for what would be essential for a man's fulfillment and satisfaction in this world.

The Formula
- Adam had a personal relationship with God
- Adam had purpose and reason for being
- Adam had a woman (Eve)

Adam had a relationship with God, meaning and significance in his life, and a woman to live and build with, all of which fulfilled his make up.

So if you want to know what it is that men really want, its God, his purpose in life, and that woman to live with. Until he has all three a man will always feel like he's chasing something and incomplete within himself. Unless a man has all three, he will feel like something…like something... ain't right. Remember, it's God, purpose, and "that" woman he wants.

He Wants God

Men naturally desire a relationship with God, like children naturally desire a relationship with their mother. Manhood is birth in the womb of God's Spirit or breath, just like a baby is birth in the womb of a mother. Therefore, men desire an intimate relationship with the Spirit of God, just like a new born baby craves it's mother's loving breast.

I hope you ladies realize that manhood is the masculine manifestation of God's purpose, principle, and presence through his male creation. Therefore, without an intimate relationship with

God, it's difficult for a man to "really" be a man.

If you happen to come into contact and form a relationship with a man that doesn't know God, you'll notice that he is always searching for something to serve. He may fall victim to the "money God", the "sex God", the "drug God", or any other element he lets master his life. But there will be a "God".

A man that doesn't know God is still a man who needs a God. Therefore, he may temporarily worship anything and devote his strength and resources to satisfy its demands. That is basically how a man's addictions work.

A man is always at the office, or on that street corner, because he worships the "money God" (He has to get all of the money). A man is always creeping with another woman, in a strip club, and can't remain faithful to one woman because he is serving the "sex God" (I need another woman and another nut). He hasn't kicked that drug or alcohol addiction because he is serving the "drug and alcohol God" (I need to get high).

Principle #21 – A man's addictions are his Gods.

I often hear women say they want a spiritual or a religious man. I question if they really understand why that is such an important quality for a man to possess. I think most women say so because it's a "text book" desire. It's just something that sounds good.

As men, we receive our direction in life from the Spirit of God. So without that direction there is a strong possibility that a man will be lost. I like to look at the male principle as the "entrepreneur" and the female principle as the "manager".

As an "entrepreneur", a man needs creative inspiration from that unseen realm. Men need to have access to more than what the natural senses can detect, in order to fully tap into their potential as men.

Men are purposed to walk with vision and direction in this world. A man's direction comes from the Spirit of God. By design, women and children can follow the lead and direction of God through a man. When a man steps into his manhood, womanhood and childhood responds accordingly.

It's easier for a woman to support (manage), with a man that knows where he's going (He's got it going on). It's easy for women and children to listen to a man that speaks wisdom. So understand that it's essential for a man to know God intimately if he is to feel connected and secure in his life. If he doesn't know the real God, he'll find one to connect with.

Understand that your man's addictions are his way of seeking the "high" and power only the Holy Spirit of God can give to him.

Remember before there was a Eve (woman), all Adam (man) had was his intimate relationship with God. So in practical terms, before he knew what it sounded like to make love to a woman, Adam knew the voice of God. Before man knew what a woman looked like, he knew God's will for his life. So before there was woman, there was God. Men really want that connection again.

Men know that they need God in their lives. They seek that relationship whether consciously or unconsciously. Men look for a God to serve, whether productively or destructively. So realize, that a man needs God in his life to feel like a man and be fulfilled. It's part of his manhood trinity.

He Wants A Purpose

A man needs a purpose, more than a fat lady needs a new heel on those worn down shoes. Purpose is power. Purpose gives meaning and significance to anything. For a man it's critical that he has meaning and significance in his life. Men need to feel apart of, or be the cause of "something" significant. Men are always looking for validation, a stamp of approval. We need to know that we count.

Men do whatever they need to do to feel "down" and to be

included. Sports, gangs, and careers, are all examples of where men seek to find their purpose and to feel apart of something significant in life.

Your man might be jumping from job to job because he is looking for his purpose in life. He may be pursuing the "wrong" things because he is looking for a meaningful association and affiliation.

Brothers are in gangs, dying in the street "game", trying to become rap stars, and well paid athletes because they are without purpose in their life. That man hanging out in sports bars with his "buddies" is getting drunk everyday because he wants to feel apart of the "club".

Men are aspiring to be the richest and most powerful men they can be because they think it will give them significance and meaning. It's a given that when a man walks in his purpose, uncommon levels of success will find him. As a result, many men choose the path of the "successful and powerful" man because he appears to be the most "prosperous". He appears to be "the man".

Have you noticed that within our inner cities, young males aspire to be one of three things in overwhelming numbers? They want to rap, play ball, or become a kingpin. It's unbelievable, but you can go into any city in this country and witness this phenomenon among the young men. That's what happens when males don't have an intimate relationship with their Creator. They will take the path of purpose the world gives, instead of walking in their own purpose, based on their gifts, passions, and personality.

If you want to see a miserable and volatile man, watch a man with no purpose for his time and body live his life. He will be the most erratic human being that he can be. Most pessimistic, hopeless, and dangerous men are those without purpose, significance, and meaning in their life.

On the other hand, if you want to see a happy, proud, and loving man, watch a man that has purpose and significance live his life. Most optimistic, positive, and generous men are those that are content in their purpose and love life.

I hope you understand that a man's purpose affects your relationship with him. How a man feels about his manhood and place in this world will affect how he treats you as his woman. If a man feels like he counts, if he feels like he has meaning, he will treat you accordingly. If a man doesn't feel like he counts, don't be surprised if he tries to discourage, abuse, and belittle your purpose.

Purpose is essential for success. Remember, God positioned Adam to "work the ground", so he had meaning in his work and with his time. Understand that Adam recognized he was making a difference in the world. He felt needed. As a result, he cheerfully welcomed Eve into his world, as a partner, someone he could share, build, and live with.

Wisdom gem* If there is no purpose for a man in your life, why would a man show up? Nothing makes a man feel better than knowing he makes a difference in his woman's world.

Principle #22 - No one needs help to accomplish nothing.

So recognize a man makes many efforts at finding his purpose and living it. Keep in mind, if Adam were never given a purpose there would have been no need for Eve (Think about that for a second).

Men desire purpose and significance in their life, more than most women are lead to believe. I actually believe that men seek purpose in their life, with the same intensity and zeal that women search for a man (Just my opinion).

I also believe that the older a man gets, the more his purpose and significance will affect his over all well being. So for all of my older and mature ladies reading this book, realize that the older a man is, the more important purpose is to his sense of manhood.

DivaGirl - How To Have A Good Man Find You

He Wants A Woman

It's a truism in life that males naturally desire females. It's also true that a man desires "that" woman in his life. When God established the manhood trinity, he blessed Adam with one woman, Eve. That one woman possessed everything Adam needed as a man from a woman.

Keep in mind at that point Adam didn't know what a woman was. Adam didn't have any "wants" from a woman. God gave Adam all that he needed. Eve was Adams perfect compliment and "helpmate". Eve was "that" woman.

Men want "that" woman in their lives. That woman who will satisfy his "needs", and compliment his "wants". Keep in mind, sex, food, and silence, are also needs (just thought I'd remind you), but there is much more to it than that.

I know you may be thinking, a man really wants one woman? I understand that it sounds like a contradiction, or just plain bullshit when all you see are men trying to get as many women as they can accumulate.

Let me tell you a little secret babygirl. That man who has all of those women is actually looking for "that" one woman in all of them. He may get good sex from Debbie. He may get love and support from Adrienne. Tammy may be his trophy, the woman that looks good on his arm. Tammy is the woman he shows off to his friends and always takes out in public. Then there may be Jackie. She is the one who causes him to think. Jackie stimulates his mind and he learns from her. Now on the surface anyone with eyes can see that this man has four different women. What is not seen, is the purpose or need that each woman satisfies for him. No one will see this man's attempt at creating "that" woman to satisfy is manhood.

When God made Eve, she was the epitome of a woman. Eve was all that God intended for her to be. So there was no need for a Debbie, Adrienne, Tammy, and Jackie. Eve was all Adam needed. Since that "fall" (Adam and Eve's death) not only has manhood suffered, but womanhood had suffered as well.

Let me tell you another little secret babygirl. The more woman that you are to your man, the less he will "need" other women. I know it may sound crazy, but its true. A man is always looking for "that" woman. So until he finds "that" woman in "one" woman, a man will have several women at one time, or all of his relationships with women will be short lived.

In many cases that "playboy" is only looking for his Eve. He is only looking for that woman who will satisfy his "secondary" wants.

After a man has an intimate relationship with God and is in his purpose, he will definitely be searching for his Eve. Have you noticed that many "successful" and "powerful" men always seem to have many women? I'll tell you once a man is "established" he needs his woman to walk through life by his side.

Even without an intimate relationship with God, or a definite purpose for his life, a man will still seek out "that" woman to be with. All heterosexual men desire their "Eve" in this world. Men seek their other rib to feel whole again. As men, we will look for that one woman who satisfies and completes our world. We are looking for our wife, the mother of our children, that lifetime partner, our "Eve". A man really wants a woman. I said a man really wants a woman, not a "ho', "bitch", "mother" or "girl", but "that" woman.

Now That I've Found Her

Once Mr. Lover has found you there are only three things your man will need from you. Keep in mind, sex, a good home cooked meal, and a peaceful residence goes without saying (Just another reminder). I want to bring your attention to three key ingredients that your man will need from you for fulfillment and satisfaction.

Remember, I told you that I was going to give you the male psyche so pay very, very close attention babygirl. Your man needs to have a position of influence in your world, your admiration, and your support. It doesn't sound like much. Now just let me explain.

Principle #23 - A man has to think like a man. He must "think" he is the man, in order to operate as a man.

Did you hear that babygirl? Your man has to think he is the man, in order to act like a man. You are probably aware of your impact, as a woman, on your man's esteem. But do you really know how influential you are to him?

It's an unknown truth to many that men are more sensitive than women are. The reason many are unaware of this truth is because men hide their emotions and sensitivity with "macho bravado". Trust me, that man is more sensitive than you would ever believe. As a result, he needs a position of influence in the relationship, he needs your admiration, and he definitely needs your support.

These Three Words

There are basically only three words that you will ever have to say as a woman for your man to feel good about himself. What do you think those three words are? Here's a hint, it's not "I love you".

If you want to see your man feel assured and take things to another level tell him, "he's the man".

There are no three words that are more empowering to manhood than those three. Men are highly sensitive and also highly logical in functioning. Therefore, he has to think himself into manhood and maximum achievement. Unlike a woman, who has to feel her way into womanhood and maximum achievement. As a woman you are a man's fuel.

Principle #24 – The man who thinks, "he is the man" will walk with confidence and dignity through any and every situation as a man.

DivaGirl - How To Have A Good Man Find You

For those of you ladies that deal with African American men realize that he may be more sensitive than the average man. Why do you think he's walking around so angry, so aggressively, and so hostile? That man is extremely sensitive and afraid of displaying that to the world.

Remember, this country has been telling and treating the Black man like "he ain't shit" for years. They have been so good with their systematic approach that not only have many Black men accepted that bullshit. I believe too many Black women and Black children have come to look at the Black man as being "shit" as well.

Understand that your words as a woman are critical to a man's confidence. After his mother's voice, a man's woman's voice is the most influential voice in his life. That is until he marries and/or has a daughter.

Women are the wind underneath every man's wings. Personally speaking, nothing gives me more motivation and inspiration as a man than my mother, sisters, and nieces. They inspire my manhood and fuel me to want to do my best.

Beware of the man whose mother always put him down and treated him like he had no value. That man tends to overcompensate for that pain she caused him. He may try to dominate women, instead of coordinate with them to feel like a man. Also beware of the man whose mother treated him like he could do no wrong. That man tends to think he's God's gift to women. He may act like he's the best thing since sliced bread. He's usually the dude with his head in his ass.

"You're the man", are the most inspirational words a man can hear, especially from his woman.

$1 Million Dollar Question

■ What do you think would happen, if you started to tell all of the men that you think, "ain't shit", that they're *"the man"*?

DivaGirl - How To Have A Good Man Find You

$Billion Dollar Answer

■ If you started to do that I guarantee that you would see their eyes brighten up, head rise, and back straighten up. You would see a complete one hundred and eighty degree transformation occur with those men.

The creative and destructive forces of life are in the words we use. The sooner you learn how to communicate, creatively (speak life) into a man, the sooner his greatness and manhood will manifest. Babygirl, your words are powerful. Your words can make or break that sensitive man.

I have a little experiment that I would like for you to participate in for me. If and when you complete it, email me (only if you want to), the details of how it turned out.

EXPERIMENT

1. Select a man that you consistently deal with. Someone that you currently think "ain't shit". He can be a babyfather, ex boyfriend, coworker, etc…
*This man will be the subject of this experiment.

2. Once you've selected your subject. I want you to write out on a blank sheet of paper three things. Fill in the blank space with your subject's name.
(Fill in the name) is in God's perfect hands. His manhood is in God's will.
(Fill in the name) is a *good man*.
(Fill in the name) is *the man*.

3. After you've created your affirmation declaration, position it where you will see it daily, for the next two weeks.

4. Read the affirmation at least once a day, twice if you have the discipline.

5. For the next two weeks, I want you to creatively speak into your subject's life. Tell him, "he's a good man", "he looks good", "he's smart", and that "good things are happening for him", etc...(You get the picture)

6. Keep a little journal monitoring you and your subject's relationship. Notice how he looks at you. Notice how he speaks to you. Notice how he treats you. Record daily, if you can. It's important that you monitor the process.

7. Also, take notice of how you feel about men in general. Also record how men are now responding to you.

I would like for you to complete the experiment and briefly email the results. I can assure you that your relationship and feelings about your subject will greatly improve. I bet that you will also see a positive change with your interactions with your subject.
More importantly, I guarantee that your relationships with men in general will improve. This experiment is for your benefit babygirl. Keep in mind, I'm showing you how to maximize your womanhood and have that good (right) man find you. So if you don't participate, it is impossible for you to celebrate. It's like the lotto, *"you have to be in to win it"*. So come on in and have some fun with the experiment. It's just for fun anyway.
Email Address: **rich@richpublications.com**

"Can I Stand There?"

There are three things your man needs from you (his Eve). They are a position of influence, your admiration, and your support.
I just explained to you just how influential your words are to his manhood. Now let me show you just how important your man's position is to him. I have a question. When you're having sex, do you prefer to be underneath your man while he controls his

strokes, or do you prefer to be on top? You can answer that now or personally show me later (That's not a joke).

Most women would prefer to be underneath their man. It's a passive and submissive position. Okay, if that question wasn't good enough how about this one. When you're going out with a man, do you prefer that he picks the place and drives or do you prefer to pick the place for the evening and drive? Once again most women would prefer to have the man select the place and drive. It's just another illustration of a woman's natural inclination to be passive and reactive in the presence of a man.

If a woman's natural tendency is to take a passive or reactive position in relation to a man. What do you think is a man's natural tendency in relation to a woman? What position do you think he would prefer?

That's right, a man prefers to be on top and in the driver's seat. Remember, a man has to think in order to act like a man. Therefore, when he is in a position of influence and control, he *thinks* he's a man. I know many of my feministic "men and women are equal" ladies out there are ready to throw something because of what I just said. Keep in mind men and women are equal but different in function.

Consider This:

Let's say we're in your car, and I'm driving us to the bookstore to pick up the other books I wrote "Punaney Galore" and "Real Men do Real Things", will we not get there at the same (equal) time? If you and I are making love, and I'm on top serving you oh so right, will not the both of us be pleased? I thought so.

A man needs some control and influence in order for him to be comfortable in a situation. If as a woman, you're very competitive, dominant, always wanting to be first, the loudest, or always wanting to be on top, it can be a catch22 for you. That attitude and spirit may work well for you in the business world, in school, or in other areas of life. However, that same spirit and attitude doesn't work well for a woman in a relationship with a man.

Keep in mind, a controlling and dominate woman is great for a "boy" looking for a "mother", but for a "man" it's a pain in the ass to cooperate with.

So are you telling me to change who I am?

Absolutely not! You might have to alter your strategy for success a bit. In order for your relationship to succeed your man needs to think and act like a man. It's the same for you. In order for your relationship to work you have to feel and act like a woman, right?

Principle #25 - A man needs to *"think like a man"* in order to act like a man, and treat a woman like a woman. A woman needs to *"feel like a woman"*, in order to act like a woman and treat a man like a man.

When you give a man some "say so", and a little authority in your world, he'll feel confident, important, and needed. When you let him "think" he's in control (we all know that women run things), he will feel like a man in the relationship. Once he begins to think and feel like a man, he'll treat you like a woman and bless your world.

A man possesses qualities that a woman doesn't possess and vice versa. So for you to be an awesome woman, your life will enhance tremendously when a man (I said a MAN), enters your blessed world. You know it's true. That's why deep down inside you crave a man to live with.

So if you want to win, pass the ball, and let your man score. Trust me you will be happy that you did. There is a beauty and power in a man that you can bring out as a woman. That's why God brought Eve to Adam. There were things in Adam that only

Eve could bring out. It's the same with you and children. Your children will bring things out of you that only they can bring out of you.

Please be clear, only give up a little control to the man that is deserving of it. Only give it to the man that shows himself to be a man. Always be wise!

I Need A Fan Club

How important are fans to a sports team, to a movie star, or to a recording artist? How do you think R. Kelly, Luther Vandross, or Mary J Blige would feel, if they gave a concert and no one showed up? How do you think Denzel Washington or Halle Berry would feel, if no one paid to see their movies? That's right, they would feel like "*shit*". They might feel unimportant. They might make a career change out of devastation.

The fans are validation and confidence builders to any performer. Now let me tell you the truth: Men are the biggest performers in the world.

Without their fans, what would happen or become of that team, that actor, entertainer, and musician. Now knowing how sensitive and performance oriented men are, what do you think would happen if a man doesn't have any fans? You better believe he'll do whatever it takes to get some.

Why do you think men buy all of those expensive ass items? The Benz, the Escalade, the jewelry, the big house, and all of that other, "look at me", a man buys and strives for, are his attempt at building a fan club. A man wants women to be on his team filling up his arena. Every man needs a fan club.

As your man's woman, as his Eve, he truly only needs you to be his biggest fan. If you are there by his side, admiring his efforts, he will excel and make you proud to be his woman. Let me tell you another secret. Men live for the admiration of women. (Like you didn't know that)

DivaGirl - How To Have A Good Man Find You

Principle #26 - Men seek the respect of their peers, approval of their elders, admiration of their woman, and affection of their children.

If you feel that in your past men have been secretive and haven't included you into their plans: It's because they didn't feel that you were supportive. If you feel like your man currently keeps you out of the loop: It's because he doesn't feel that you are his fan.

If your man doesn't feel like you are his "fan", understand that he is getting "fan recognition" from another source. If you are not your man's number one fan, please believe another woman is. If you are always shooting down his plans, ideas, or suggestions, trust that there is, or will be, some other woman giving him what he needs. Sorry baby I didn't make the rules but still respect the game.

Remember, you agreed that without the fans validation, even Mary J Blige might stop singing. So how do you think your man will feel because of your lack of support and encouragement?

We've all heard the Black woman's complaint about interracial dating and marriages. They say that, "White women are always getting all the rich and successful brothers". Now let me hit you with a logical situation.

If men are performance oriented. If all performers need support to succeed, and if "white" women have been perceived to be the biggest supporters. What would be the next logical conclusion?

I'm here to tell you no man is rich and successful without support. I don't know why it appears that many rich and successful Black men are dating and marrying White women. My guess is, maybe the brother had a negative experience with a few Black women in his early development. He was probably in a verbally abusive relationship (A trait we picked up from slavery) with a Black woman. As a result, he stereotyped all Black women to be loud, disrespectful, and verbally abusive. It happens all of the time people have a negative experience with one person and then stigmatize a whole group of people.

If a Black man didn't grow up with Black women (his mother, sisters, aunts, etc) being his "fans", he might take the OJ Simpson route. I personally don't have anything against interracial relationships.

If a man connects with the right woman and she satisfies his needs, or if a woman connects with the "right" man then more power to them. I just want to inform you babygirl, your man needs you to be his biggest fan.

So hold him down. Let him know that you want the best for him in every way possible. Remember, whatever you give you receive multiplied, if given to the right source. So be your man's number one fan and watch him return the love in a "manly way".

Give Me A Cheer

Do you cheer your man on? Are you in his corner encouraging his efforts? When your man looks at you is he being inspired to be more and to accomplish greater things? It's a fact that in this country African American women aren't perceived and assumed to be much of a cheerleader for the Black man.

I'm aware of the fact that many Black men aren't deserving of cheers. Many of us are into the wrong things. And it would be foolish to support a foolish attempt. But when you really think about it, that man who is on the wrong track and into the wrong things needs love and support more than anyone else.

Earlier on I briefly explained to you just how sensitive men are and Black men in particular. Now let me ask you a simple question. In order for your man to go to another level, what do you think is required first, a "better performance" on his part, or your "cheers and support"? Obviously that's a trick question because it's a little bit of both. He needs to perform better and he also needs your support.

As an athlete and huge sports fan let me share some of my

experience with you. The fans and the cheerleaders inspire intensity, hard work, hustle, and greatness out of an athlete and team. Your man needs your cheers badly and unfortunately he won't ask for them. For some reason men don't ask for what they want (specifically), but we seek it until we find it. So don't expect to hear your man say, "I need your encouragement and support baby."

Some men will ask for help but the majority of us won't. Just keep in mind he needs it anyway. Remember, if he can't get a cheer and some support from you, he'll go find it from someone else.

For all of you single ladies, become a fan and cheerleader of the men you currently know (Especially your sons). Once you start cheering all men on, watch how your fortune with all men will improve. Whether you believe it or not a man measures the majority of his effectiveness as a man based on a woman.

Man's Measurement Test

- How many women can I get?
- Am I satisfying her in bed?
- Can I get her to fall in love with me?
- Will she be there no matter what happens?

If a man feels successful in those areas he'll be confident in his manhood, well as far as the ladies are concerned. As a man finds his Eve and matures in his manhood, he'll measure his effectiveness as a man in less egotistical ways. But until then he will be very egotistical. I bring all of this to your attention just to show you how significant you are to a man.

Don't you ever let a few disrespectful assholes influence you to think that men don't respect woman. In fact, men not only respect women, many of us men *fear* women more than anything in this world. Why do you think men operate on so much ego instead of according to the heart? Why do you think it takes a man so long to commit his heart to a woman? He's scared.

Trust me, many men fear the influence of women on their lives. We don't want to look soft, whipped, or sprung out because of love and a women's power on us.

Plus, we're extra sensitive on top of being scared... forget about it. That's why so many of us are a mess.

Hopefully, you can now see your importance as a woman to a man. As a woman you can cheer your man onto greater heights and levels. He can go from an inmate to the prison's warden. He can go from being a highschool drop out to a Harvard professor. He can go from having ten dollars to being worth millions of dollars because of your cheers. Trust me, a man with a supportive and strong woman by his side cannot be denied. Cheer him on and watch him support you. Cheer him on and watch you two achieve great things together.

Conclusion

That's it. That is all men want. Men are very simple functioning creatures. We basically want the same thing women want, LOVE. We are all human beings that all desire the blessings of God in life. Your man wants love more than he can articulate. The difference between you and him is that he perceives his sensitivity as weakness and being unmanly. So he won't ask for help submissively but will cry out for help aggressively and with his behavior.

When a man cries out for help, it looks like anger, fear, disrespect, and with addictions. Just remember a call is still a call.

Key Points to Remember
- Man is primarily looking for three things
    1). A personal relationship with God
    2). His purpose in life
    3). "That" woman in his life (his Eve)

■   A man has to "think" he is a man in order to "act" like a man.

■   Men are simple but sensitive creatures that are not that good at articulating their need for love.

■   A man wants three pivotal things from a woman
        1). A position of authority, control, and influence
        2). Admiration (fan club)
        3). Support (cheerleader)

BONUS
Sex (including oral), a good meal, peace and quiet are also important to a man but then again they are to you too.

CHAPTER 9

MR. IDEAL vs MR. REAL: NO MORE BULLSHIT

"How come you're so positive about men? You act like they can do no wrong." *The young and inexperienced woman said to the wise lady, as they sat having tea.* *"Is that what you believe that I'm positive because I think men can do no wrong?"* *Asked the wise lady, as she poured some tea.* *"That's exactly what I think. I watch you everyday and you're at peace with every man you know. Your husband, your brothers, and your sons can do no wrong in your eyes. Why is that?"* *The inexperienced woman asked desperately, shaking her head in amazement.* *"It's not that they can do no wrong in my eyes. For we all miss it from time to time. I've learned how to be patient with their immaturity. I've learned how to listen for their needs. I also learned how to forgive them for their wrongs."* *The wise woman answered with a peaceful smile on a radiant face.* *"But...but why do you do it? Men are such jerks. If you give them an inch, they'll want a yard."* *The inexperienced woman said angrily.* *"I do so because long ago, I was immature, I once didn't know how to communicate my needs, and I still do wrong from time to time. Besides, I do it because I'm not dead yet..."*

Wise Lady and Inexperienced Woman

INTRODUCTION

What is the moral of that story? If you have to read it again and again until you can take away something from it. Do so because there is a moral to it.

Now let me share with you the moral of that story. As long as you're still living in your physical body, life will ask you to grow up, to listen, to be understanding, and to forgive. The moral is, as long as you're still living in your physical temple you and Mr. Perfect won't meet.

The only perfect men in this world are laid down six feet deep in some dirt, at a gravesite.

Okay, now that I've hit you with that dose of the truth, describe on a separate sheet of paper your "ideal man".

Now let me ask you a very simple question. Have you met your ideal man yet? For those of you that don't know what an ideal is let me explain. An ideal is a concept of something as perfect. It's a standard of perfection or excellence, according to the American Heritage Concise Dictionary.

So have you and Mr. Perfect met? I'll bet five thousand dollars that you haven't met Mr. Perfect. Don't be surprised that I'm betting against you babygirl. I look at it like this. If you have already met Mr. Perfect, then why are you reading this book? (Simple logic)

Now for those of you that do have significant others, I have something to say. It isn't Mr. Ideal that you are dealing with. Your man isn't Mr. Perfect, but Mr. Reality right? So please tell these other ladies to leave the Mr. Ideal for the novels, movies, and fairy tales.

Guess Who Mr. Ideal Really Is?

Mr. Ideal ain't who you think he is? Trust me, once you find out who he is you're going to be very disappointed. It's not a surprise to me that Mr. Ideal hasn't come around, riding on that white horse to sweep you off of your feet. To my knowledge Mr. Ideal doesn't even ride horses.

So where have you been so far in your quest to find Mr. Ideal? Have you put on your prom dress and went to church thinking he would be there? Did you put on your "ho suit" and go to the club thinking he would be in the VIP? Is he at the office? Is he in your class or on campus? How long have you been looking for this man? Has it been days, months, or years that you've been on the hunt? Doesn't it seem that no matter what you do or where you go he's never there?

The brother you met at church turned, out to be a "playa". The brother from the club, was Al Bundy (married with children). Todd, from the office, doesn't make enough money. The brother your girl Pam hooked you up with turned out to be bisexual. So what's the deal divagirl? How come after all of your efforts, you haven't found him? Your ex-boyfriends and baby's father(s) turned out to be bad deals and bad calls. So what's really good? What's really going on?

If you calmly sit back and think about it, Mr. Ideal has to be the hardest man in the world to find. Do you know why, no matter where you look, or what you do you'll never find him? Now get ready babygirl because I might disgust you with what I'm about to say. Are you ready? Okay now here it is. The reason why Mr. Ideal hasn't shown up yet is because, Mr. Ideal is....... ***YOU.***

What Do You Mean, "He's Me"?

The reason why Mr. Ideal wasn't at church that Easter Sunday you went to church. The reason why Mr. Ideal wasn't at the club that night you had your shank outfit on (I was there I saw you). The reason why he's never at the office no matter who they hire is because Mr. Ideal lives in your head. Mr. Ideal doesn't have a body. The man doesn't walk among us everyday men in the world. Divagirl all of this time you've been looking for Mr. Ideal out in the world, but he's lives upstairs in your head. (On the fifth floor)

DivaGirl - How To Have A Good Man Find You

Mr. Ideal is you and your concepts of the perfect man. I never understood why people are so insecure about another man or woman ruining their relationship, when it has been Mr. and Mrs. Ideal doing the job. What you don't believe me? You think I'm sitting here lying to you? Okay now let me tell you how Mr. Ideal operates. Let me put you on to his MO.

Mr. Ideal's Modioperandi (MO)

*Mr. Ideal thinks he is always right.
*Mr. Ideal thinks everyone needs to improve but him.
*Mr. Ideal will always tell you "he's not enough", referring to another man.
*Mr. Ideal wants you to think, "the grass is greener" for your girlfriends, for that married woman, etc...
*Mr. Ideal wants to be the only man you know.

Don't Believe "Him"!

Mr. Ideal sits up in your head and will ruin your relationships if you allow him to. He'll tell you all types of things about the men that show up in your life. Have you ever heard this from Mr. Ideal, "He's not tall enough, smart enough, funny enough?" Has Mr. Ideal ever told you that another man doesn't have enough education or money to be with you?

What has Mr. Ideal said to you about that man who has been to jail, or about that man who doesn't go to church? What has he said about that man who "still" lives at home with his mother?

Mr. Ideal is a *"playa hater"* for real, for real. If you're not conscious of what Mr. Ideal is telling you he'll successfully ruin your prospects with men. He'll have your walking around with your neck all stiff and nose up in the air, like you're "better" than someone. Like I said, Mr. Ideal wants to be the only man you know. He wants you single, alone, and waiting for him to come along. He wants you, reading those fairytale romance novels and watching those unrealistic love stories, increasing his influence on your life.

The funny thing is Mr. Ideal ain't coming. It's a set up. Mr. Ideal will have you proud, unforgiving, impatient, and extremely unrealistic about other men. If you want to be happy don't listen to Mr. Ideal, because Mr. Ideal is a fraud.

Mr. Ideal wants you to think that he is right around the corner. That way, you'll give up on the men you know. Mr. Ideal is imaginative but very real at the same time. If you want a good man to find you my advice is to kill Mr. Ideal right now. If you want to bring the good out of the man you have now then stop cheating on him with Mr. Ideal. In fact, do me a favor, kill Mr. Ideal right now.

Go get the gun that's hidden in your Prada shoebox and shoot him dead. Go ahead, let me hear the gun pop. Oh, I'm sorry baby. I almost forgot that Mr. Ideal is you. I don't want to have you killing yourself (I just lost it for a second). Please understand that Mr. Ideal has to be dealt with.

Mr. Real Is All There Is

How many times have you met someone and they didn't turn out to be who you thought or assumed they would be? Remember the guy that you thought was fine. Didn't he turn out to be an asshole? In the beginning didn't you think he was going to be the smoothest and best lover in the world?

*It happens to me all of the time. I meet a lovely lady that I initially think, "Is all of that". Then after a short while something else settles in. She goes from being "that" (the one) woman who has all of my attention, to just "another" woman. Has that ever happened to you? (Maybe it's just a man thing)

Have you ever met someone and you were all excited, thinking they were "that" one. Then come to find out they were just "another" one. After much introspection, I've come to a conclusion. When we first meet someone we project our "ideals"

*This section was written before I met and married my wife

onto them. Then after we get to know them a stronger force called… *"Reality"*, settles in. I'm sure you would love to meet that "perfect" man. Unfortunately the "perfect" man doesn't exist.

The good news in life is we don't need to find the "perfect" mate. Therefore, you don't need Mr. Perfect to come sweep you up off of your feet. All you need is the "right" man in your life.

In reality divagirl, you may have it going on, but you're not **"ALL** of that". In reality I may be a good catch but I'm not Mr. Perfect. We all have strengths and weakness, we are all knowledgeable of some things and ignorant of much more. The truth is we all have some learning, growing, and living to do. As a result, no one out here is "all of that". Mr. and Mrs. Ideal are false, Mr. and Mrs. Real is all there is.

Don't misunderstand or underestimate what I'm saying. Mr. Real is actually a better option and match for you than Mr. Ideal could ever be. Mr. Real is your man for four reasons:

> Mr. Real forces you to **Learn**
> Mr. Real forces you to **Stretch** (experience)
> Mr. Real forces you to **Grow**
> Mr. Real causes you to **Love**

The School Of Hard Knocks

Do you want to hear something funny? Did you know that all of the men in your past served the same purpose?

Would you believe that every man from your past was a teacher? Every last one of them showed up in your life at the time they did in order to teach you something.

$Million Dollar Question
■ What were they there to teach me?

$Billion Dollar Answer
■ They were to teach you how to love, live, and be yourself.

Through all of your experiences with men what have you learned? Have you learned that it always pays to be true to your essence, instead of pretending to be someone else? Have you learned how to be forgiving, instead of walking around with bitterness? Are you now understanding because of your past? Did that one nightstand with "what's his name" teach you to slow down? Did your baby's father teach you to use birth control? I sure hope you've learned some "how to's" and not only the "not to's", from your past experiences with men?

I hope that after all you've been through you now know how to listen. I hope you now know how to communicate your wants and needs, effectively to a man (Remember it's different than talking to your girls).

If you haven't learned anything from your experiences, don't be surprised if you continue to go through the same situations. Don't be surprised if your new boyfriend has the same tendencies as your last man. Until you learn what it is you need to learn, life and love will continue to ask you the same questions. It won't matter if it takes Chris, Shawn, Dennis, or Paul, to bring the question (situations) to you. Until you answer correctly you won't progress and move on. The school of hard knocks is serious and it's always in session.

Stretching Is Good For You

Do you know what happens to muscles if they aren't stretched and pressured (exercised)? They weaken and fall victim to fat (We all know that fat saps energy and energy is necessary for effort). Do you realize that all the men you've dealt with and all of the men you are dealing with are to make you stronger? Do you notice that men are always causing you to stretch?

How many times have you and your man had a misunderstanding? How many times has something happened in your relationship that you thought would never happen to you (divorce, unwanted pregnancy, etc)?

Think about all of the times you've done things that at first you were against doing. You have definitely been stretched babygirl. Wouldn't you say that you are a much stronger (not bitter) woman today, than you were five years ago? Of course you are.

I personally prefer to be with an African American woman for one reason. Living in this country has forced the both of us to stretch and develop our character (If we are positive). I know that any woman, especially a Black woman that can walk with her head up in this country is a strong (character) woman. Nothing against all of the sexy Latin, White, and Asian ladies out there. Trust me I love y'all as well.

I hope you accept the fact that men will cause you to stretch. Men are going to put you into uncomfortable and pressured situations. It's not because men are difficult or because men are assholes. It's because as a woman, men are going to be some of your greatest teachers.

Just think about how much you've already learned from this book. Did you forget that it was a man who wrote it? (That would be me). Men will stretch you out babygirl, whether you like it or not. So don't expect everything to be "peachy creamy". This is the real world.

Growing Up

Are you the same height and weight now that you were at ten or fifteen years old? Of course not. Physically we can all see your growth and maturity. Your chest and behind has filled out. (I bet it looks good on you) Your voice has changed as well. If we were to look at your pictures we would all be able to see that you have changed physically. And now you have that lovely body.

So has the rest of you grown up as well. Do you still act like a twelve year old when you don't get your way?

Have you also grown mentally, emotionally, and with your character? Do you still think about yourself, men, and relationships the same way you did at sixteen? I pray that you don't. I hope that you've changed and grown in a positive way. I hope all of the experience you've gained with men hasn't been in vain.

I hope you realize that you grow mentally through expanding and strengthening your thoughts. You grow emotionally by expanding your range or emotions. Contrary to your childhood experience there are more than the happy and sad emotions to express. Your character grows through challenge. That's why some men you've encountered have been so difficult for you to get along with. It's because of challenge that you went through what you've gone through.

So ask yourself, am I a better woman because of what I've been through? Is your character stronger as a result of the challenges in your life? After the pain and heart break of those failed relationships, are you wiser now?

Change is the key to growth. As a result of your experience, are you a changed woman. It may be a fact that you didn't enjoy everything you've been through with men but here you stand today a new woman because of it.

The older you become, the more changes you will go through. Therefore, you have to realize and come to grips with the fact that your body will change, your feelings will change, your opinions will change, your goals, and your desires will change as well. It's important that you come to grips with this. If you are stuck on ideals, *"who"* you want today, might not be *"who"* you want tomorrow.

Men don't only show up in your life to make you happy and to cater to your superficial wants. One of the main reasons why men show up in your life is to cause you to change and grow as a woman. Men will make you a better (not bitter) woman divagirl if you allow them to.

I Would Like To Meet You

Would you believe me if I said you have a program inside

of you that selects your men for you? Whether you believe me or not it's the absolute truth.

You have an internal program that determines the men that will show up in your life. Your program determines who your Mr. Real will be. Have you ever wondered why you attract the type of men that you do into your life? Why when you're looking for Mr. Ideal (perfect), Tyrone and his drama shows up? You can sit up all night and think about the man you "want", but you continue to hook up with what you "get". Why is that?

Let me tell you what's going on right now. You keep attracting the men that you are attracting for three simple reasons:

Three Reasons of Attraction
> Because of who you are
> Because of what you need
> Because of what you expect

Who You Are

Earlier, I showed you the seven relational styles. I now want to take it one step further. Who you are is the most important element to your world. When I say who you are, I'm referring to that identification space right outside of your core. I don't believe that people actually tap into who they really are, unless they know who God is. I also don't believe that many of us know God. I think many of us "believe in a God" but many of us don't "know God".

If we did tap into who we really are, this world would light up with love. I believe people would be more purposeful, prosperous, and supernaturally powerful if we walked according to who we "truly" are.

When I say that identification space that exist right outside of your core self, I'm not talking about the "real" you. Your self-image, self esteem, and self worth make up that identification space. I actually call that identification space your "self-concept".

DivaGirl - How To Have A Good Man Find You

Your self-concept is the most influential force in your life. It determines the quality of your life. Many people believe that God is the most influential force in their lives. But that's not true and here's why: God doesn't need you to be positive or powerful, in order for him to be God and to fulfill his Will. God will always be God regardless of who you choose to be.

On the other hand, you need to have a healthy and positive self-concept to be powerful and accomplished in this world. As a result, you can have "faith in God", and not have faith in your own gifts, talents, and abilities, and "miss" God. So never underestimate the power of your self- concept. Who you are determines your life's capacity.

The key to a healthy self-concept is to destroy any and everything that is a contaminant to your identity. The "bitch" and "ho", or any other false association you have must be put to rest immediately. A "ho's" capacity is much smaller than a "woman's" capacity. That's why I encourage that you step into your womanhood boldly.

If you don't embrace your womanhood it will be difficult for a man to show up in your world. If you're not all the woman you can be, you won't be able to handle all that a man brings into your world. A man will be too much for you to deal with if you're less than a woman.

The beautiful thing is, life is fair. God will never give you more than you can handle. You will never attract anyone not in harmony with who you are. So if all you are accustomed to dealing with are "little boys", "players". "jerks", or whatever name you call the men that show up in your life, what does that say about you?

If he's a "little boy" then what are you? Remember we manifest what we are.

What You Need

When are you ladies gonna understand that every man you

177

connect with in life isn't meant to become a boyfriend, a sex partner, or a husband? There are other reasons why you and Lance hit it off so well at the office. You didn't have to sleep with Greg because he was there for you when your lights got turned off. Men will come into your world for a number of reasons. The main reason being they are there to teach you something.

Many times men will show up in your life because you have a life lesson to learn. Men will also show up because you need some male companionship. Brothers will show up because you may need some financial assistance, some encouragement, or because you need a positive male influence for your son or daughter.

There are many needs that you have which men will show up in your life to satisfy. You must understand that a "romantic" or "committed" relationship might be something that you "want", but it might not be something that you "need" at the time.

I hope you can see just how destructive Mr. Ideal is to your relationships. Mr. Ideal will have you shutting down a brother that was coming into your world to be a "friend", just because he doesn't have a million dollars. Mr. Ideal will have you turn down a man that was coming to be a force of encouragement to your world, just because he isn't a GQ model.

Men will show up to satisfy your "needs". Don't limit the possibility of "why" a man shows up in your life. Realize that Mr. Ideal will never show up, even though he say's he will. What you "need" is a strong factor in determining who you will connect with in life.

If you "need" to learn how to trust, watch a former "playboy" show up with all of his "history" and rock your world. If you "need" to learn how to give, watch that brother show up that needs a lot of assistance from you. Whatever it is that you "need", will be a strong indicator in who you will "need".

I strongly recommend that you come to grips with the fact that who you "want", might not satisfy "who" you "need". Therefore, "who" you "need", will always be there in life, despite "who" you "want".

DivaGirl - How To Have A Good Man Find You

What You Expect

Let me show you just how funny some of you ladies are. How can you say that you "want" Mr. Ideal to show up, but then expect Mr. Ordeal to come knocking? Do you remember the first chapter of this book? Why do you think I opened with a chapter entitled "All men are good"?

I feel that too many of you ladies have low expectations of men.

"Men are dogs", "niggas ain't shit", "you can't trust no "man", are all things that women say and believe about men, right? Understand, that another reason why you connect with certain men is because they confirm your beliefs and expectations regarding men.

If you believe that "*niggas ain't shit*" and expect that a man is "*drama*", watch who shows up. Troy will show up with his three baby mothers, without a job, and some court dates on his hand asking for your love and support. Troy will only be confirming your expectations. It's what you expected anyway, right?

Now, it's not my style to keep creating negative hypothetical situations, so let me flip the script. What do you think would happen if you believed that "all men are good" and expected men to improve your quality of life? That's right, you will connect with those brothers that confirm your beliefs and expectations.

It's What You Don't See

I hope you're picking up on the theme of this book. It's that which goes on in the inside of you that determines what happens on the outside of you. Mr. Ideal is a man you've created that lives on the <u>inside</u> of you, but he ruins your <u>outside</u>. Mr. Real is a man who lives on the <u>outside</u> but is determined by your <u>inside</u>. Who you are, what you "need", and what you expect determines who your Mr. Real will be in life.

I know that many of you ladies are stuck on how "good" a

man looks, with what he drives, where he works, etc…
Understand, that you are perfectly entitled to your preferences.
That's your business.

If you prefer a man that is six feet or taller, that's okay. If
you prefer that a man has some financial stability; that's
understandable. I just hope you realize it's what you don't see that
supercedes your preferences. What I mean is this. Someone can
look good on paper, meaning they meet all of your preferences to a
tee. Yet there is a possibility that you two still might not make a
meaningful connection.

Rob can be fine, have a nice job, and be hung like a
horse... and still not fulfill you. Who you are, what you "need", and
what you expect are the magnetic forces of a relationship. For
those of you ladies that "want" to get married. Do you understand
that you have to be married on the inside before you marry on the
outside?

*   What do you mean be married on the inside?

In order to get married you have to be a wife on the inside
first. You have to accept the responsibilities of what you desire
mentally and emotionally before you possess it physically. The
mental and emotional levels of a "wife" and a "girlfriend" are two
different levels. The physical reality of a wife and girlfriend are
also different.

If all you've ever been in your relationship is a
"girlfriend", what does that say to you? It says to me that all
you've been connecting to were "boyfriends" for one. Secondly, it
suggests that if you want to go to the next level of "wife" and
marriage you'll have to grow mentally and emotionally.

Principle #28 – All growth requires change.

There is a common dynamic that happens in men and
women relationships. They both start out on a "boyfriend and

girlfriend", or "man and woman" level mutually. Then the change occurs.

Being that women are more relational than men, women tend to outgrow that initial level faster than the man. Then a woman starts to "want more" (Sound familiar).

Being that men are more positional than women, "more" for a man means, more obligations and responsibilities (It's like a job). So he is slower with his development and might not "want more", right now. The woman then takes his "not right now", as a "never", and she goes to work.

She either works to change his "not right now" into a "let's get married", or she works to change his "not right now" into a "let's get married". I'm not implying that women are manipulative or tricky. I am saying that women have a stronger tendency to work at bringing a relationship to their level of satisfaction than men do.

If a woman is a "wife", yet her man is still a "boyfriend", she can influence him to marry her and bring the relationship to her level of satisfaction. Well at least physically, meaning they have all of the "titles".

Principle #29 - Men lead with directions, women lead by suggestion.

Now let me ask you a serious question Ms. Lady? What do you think is going to happen if a "wife" and a "boyfriend" marries? That marriage will be miserable for that married woman and her married "boyfriend". Remember, it's what you don't see that controls what you see. A man can put a ten carat platinum and diamond rock on your finger on your wedding day, and still be a "boyfriend" mentally and emotionally, when he says "I do" at the alter. Like I said a woman can influence a relationship physically, but the mental and emotional is up to each individual.

Maybe the divorce rate wouldn't be so high, if only "husbands" and "wives" got married. Think about that for a moment. Check yourself for a second. Have you been asking for more than you can successfully handle? Are you a "girlfriend", asking for marriage?

Have you tried to persuade your "boyfriend" into marriage because it is something that you wanted? I need you to keep it real with me. Have you been trying to get blood from a rock? I'm here to tell you the truth. Your "boyfriend", will make a terrible "husband", and you will make a terrible "wife", as a "girlfriend".

I personally think that's why marriage has such a bad look today. There are so many "boyfriends and girlfriends, "mothers and sons", and "fathers and daughters" getting married. Let's leave the marriage thing for the "husbands and wives" okay. Keep in mind what I'm referring to is the mental and emotional capacity as well as the relational style, of an individual.

So if you want to marry Mr. Real, step up your "game" and become a "wife". Remember it's the inside that determines the outside. A wife is the supreme relational position for a woman. It's the big leagues. It's for professionals only.

Principle #30- It's who you are that influences what you do, what you do sets the stage for what you have. What you have (experience) perputuates what you expect.

Don't Fear Change

Be prepared, I might disrupt your whole way of thinking right now. If how you've been thinking and if what you've been doing hasn't been successful, will you change your thinking and doing in order to be effective? Many of you won't because change is a very uncomfortable transition and an awkward emotional state to go through.

Remember when you went from crawling to walking (Well maybe you don't)? I know you remember when you first learned how to ride a bike. Do you recall how the awkarness and uncomfort of not knowing felt? In order to grow you must change.

DivaGirl - How To Have A Good Man Find You

In order to change you must go through a transition. Remember you had to <u>learn</u> how to ride that bike, and to learn you had to <u>change</u>. Going into a new form or a new situation can be frightening, but it's something we've all been through.

I hope you understand if you internally grow from being a "girlfriend" into a "wife" during the course of your relationship, you'll experience some awkwardness as well. Especially if you're still seeing Mr. Ideal (remember him). If you grow within a relationship and it isn't mutual, you'll outgrow the relationship with your "boyfriend". (He'll really start to get on your nerve) You'll want *"more"* and he won't be ready for *"all of that"*.

Now if there wasn't so much of yourself invested into that relationship, it would be easy for you to see and accept the fact that you have to move on. But that's not how it really works in life. In the real world we hang onto relationships we have outgrown, because we fear the unknown and are comfortable.

Wisdom gem* It's perfectly natural and okay to outgrow a relationship (situation). Keep in mind that you don't outgrow people. But you can outgrow the relationship with that person.

Never fear moving on, if it calls for it. Your soul and spirit must always be free, in order for you to prosper peacefully in life. If you're in a relationship with Keith, and you two "find" love together, that is special. However, you can still love Keith and outgrow the relationship (situation), with him. I believe that one of the reasons why people aren't as prosperous, successful, and happy as they can be, is because they are still attached to old things.

The number one thing that you need to let go of in order to be successful, is Mr. Ideal. He is never coming. If you outgrow your relationship with Keith, don't fear the change of moving on. If you become a "wife", in order to be successful you need a "husband" (Do you get it). Therefore, you can still love Keith, and he not be the "husband" you "need". Remember, you may *prefer* that Keith be your "husband", but you may *need* "Steve" to be.

Who you are, what you need, and what you expect, supercedes your preferences. Don't fear the change of growth if you want more out of life.

$Million Dollar Question

■   So are you saying, that if me and my man aren't on the same level that I "should" leave him?

$10 Million Dollar Answer

■   No, that's not what I said. I am saying that if you two grow and develop at a different pace, the relationship will begin to feel awkward and send you through some changes. I am saying that if you start "wanting more", maybe another situation (relationship) is needed. I am saying, never fear moving on if need be. Life only gets better as you move forward. If you are honest with yourself and do the "right" things, you will grow and be prosperous.

<u>Conclusion</u>

Are you now convinced that Mr. Ideal is nothing more than your ego? He doesn't really exist. He is not on his way, divagirl. I don't care what he tells you. Mr. Real is the man for you. Mr. Real is who you will know on a everyday basis. Mr. Real will be your "friend", your "boyfriend", and your "man".

It's perfectly normal to have your preferences. In fact it's healthy. Just never allow your preferences to rate your men for you, or to deceive you into thinking you are better than anyone.

We all have lessons to learn. So lighten up and learn to love. Mr. Ideal is a fraud, a figment of your imagination. He will never be someone you deal with physically (He's an idea). Mr. Ideal wants you disrespecting and undervaluing the men you currently know.

Mr. Ideal wants you thinking that you are too good for the brother who does security in your office building. Mr. Ideal wants you thinking that you are too pretty for the heavyset brother who sits next to you in class (The one that treats you like a lady). Kill Mr. Ideal and allow Mr. Real to live and increase the joy and happiness in your world.

Key Points To Remember

■   Mr. Ideal is not that brother you have your eyes on in church, leading the choir, or sipping Moet in the club, or that handsome dude around campus. Mr.Ideal is actually a woman, because Mr. Ideal is **YOU**.

■   Mr. Real and his strengths and weakness will be your man.

■   Who you are, what you 'need", and what you expect (believe) about men determines who your Mr. Real will be.

■   Embrace any connection you make with a man because he could be there to satisfy one of your "needs".

■   Only one man will be your "husband" so there's no need to pressure every man, especially your life's "boyfriends" into marriage.

■   Never fear the changes of growth. Life only gets better.

Special Note

I really hope this chapter freed you from the strongholds of Mr. Ideal. I pray that you are now free to talk to anyone (just talk with), that politely speaks to you. I pray that you are now free to dance (just dance), in the club with that dude who steps to you correctly. I hoped I killed all of the snobbish and bitchy ways that many of you were walking around with, before reading this book.

Remember you have it going on but you are not "all of that" babygirl. So treat people like human beings. Especially the men that properly approach you, even if they are not what you prefer. Remember Mr. Ideal isn't coming to sweep you off of your feet. So why not step off of your high horse.

Mr. Real is the man that is going to love you, hold you close, challenge you, ask you to marry him, father your children, make love to you, talk to you, get on your nerve, disappoint you, frustrate you, hurt you, forgive you, misunderstand you. Mr. Real, is going to make you smile, make you feel good, make you cry, impress you, surprise you. Mr. Real is the real and all that it brings. Mr. Real is all there is.

CHAPTER 10

LET A MAN BE A MAN

"This is a man's world...but it wouldn't be nothing without a woman or girl."

James Brown

INTRODUCTION

This is personally going to be my favorite chapter in the book. I know I've probably said that before, but this is my favorite chapter, for real for real. I truly believe that this chapter alone is worth the price of this book. "Let a man be a man".

Once again, I want to communicate to your soul and spirit. I want to touch your inside. I want to get all up in ya (Ha, ha). Seriously speaking, I want to talk the talk again babygirl. Let me start by asking you a few questions. Do you appreciate men? Do you honor and respect what God has put into the male body? Do you accept the fact that men are different from you as a woman? Do you really accept that?

I hope that by now many of your false beliefs about men are dead. If they're not, reread this book over and over until the light comes on.

Did you know that womanhood is birth out of manhood? I'm quite sure that you didn't forget Eve came from out of Adam, right? You do understand that it was your father, that sent you through your mother (physically)? You didn't forget any of that, right?

You do realize that when men aren't men, women suffer? I hope you realize that the biggest problem in this country, especially within the Black community, is manlessness.

Yet despite all of that, do you cherish the power of God in men? I can just hear some of you saying, "**Hell No!**" The thought of a man being the reason why you are here might be disturbing to the "feminist" and "man basher" in you.

Remember, I really don't care how you feel about what I'm saying. As long as it's all in love, I'm good. I'm not trying to hurt you (just love you) baby.

Men Have It Going Too!

Men have it going on in their own special way too. A man will bring to your life only that which a man can bring. I realize that it might appear as if men have forgotten what being a man is all about. I know many of us men, walk around like we don't even know our names (Many don't, his name isn't PeeWee). Yet underneath all of that confusion men have it going on.

It disgusts me to see so many men wanting to be pretty. It hurts me to see men "trying" to be beautiful; having long braids down their backs, wearing more diamonds than their mother and woman put together, and getting their feet and nails done (My personal pet peeve). It pains me to see so many brothers acting like "niggas" and "suckers", being weak, docile, and ignorant.

The next nonfiction book that I release will be on the subject of manhood. So be on the lookout. Don't forget to buy at least three copies, buy one for yourself, and two more to pass on to some men that you love. I promise that the book will be a classic (promotion).

Men are more than your eyes can reveal. Black men are more than "jailbirds", "athletes", "father runners", "playboys", or any of that other stereotypical shit we are called today. That brother in jail, those brothers lost to the streets, and that man struggling to make ends meet, can rock your entire world if he would just step into his manhood.

If he would accept what God has made him and apply the principles and truths of God's Word to his life… forget about it. He would have your toes curling, heart skipping beats, and temperature rising as he enters a room.

I've encouraged womanhood, being a lady, and success all throughout this book. It's now time that we understand and honor the man. Besides, why would you want to be with someone that you thought, didn't have it going on?

A Man Is A Man

A **Man is a Man**. Read that statement fifty times if you need to for it to register into your system. I didn't say that a "man is a woman". I didn't say that, "a man is your girlfriend." I said a man is a man. I make a conscious effort to make statements that will arrest your criminal beliefs. So many of your beliefs have been committing murder, killing your possibilities of having a great relationship with Mr. Lover.

How long have you been judging and evaluating men, based on your woman standards? How many times have you compared your father to your mother? How often do you judge you and your man's friendship, based on you and your girlfriend Pam's?

Wisdom gem* It's not profitable for you to talk to your man in the same fashion that you talk to your girlfriends, mothers, sisters, aunts, or any other woman for that matter. You can tell them both the same things, just not the same way.

Your man is different from every woman you know and here's why. Your man or a man is not your mother, your grandmother, your aunt, your girlfriends, your sister, your sorority sisters, etc... That **Man is a Man.**

If a man is like the women you know, *beware*. That man must be light in his ass. That man might be a sweetheart. (Ha, ha, ha, ha, ha...)

For the most part it's easy to distinguish a man from a woman physically. I don't think that is where our problem rests. I think we don't comprehend mentally and emotionally that we are dealing with the compliment (not opposite) sex in our relationships. In our relationships, I think we take it for granted that our partner is of a different function than us. Keep that in mind the next time you get into a difficult situation with a man. Keep in mind that a man is man.

A man, might not understand where you are coming from with your "woman's world". You might not understand his "man's world". But you both can seek to understand each other. So accept the fact that a man is a man and not a wo-man.

A man may be a terrible woman, but he's got it going on as a man. A man is strong, he loves his woman, he has direction, and he wants a woman. A man is a man.

A Man Thinks Like A Man

I want to share with you a deep deep secret about men. Are you ready? Okay here it is. Men really don't care that much for detail. Consequently, if you're talking to a man and you want to be effective with your message, all you have to do is one thing....
GET TO THE F#@%ING POINT!

Principle #32 - A man's question is "*what?*" a woman's question is "*why?*"

Men want to know "what" the bottom line is of any message. Men are not big on detail. We want the big picture. It's not that men are inconsiderate of feelings. A man's make up is very logical, so we need to *SEE* the picture.

DivaGirl - How To Have A Good Man Find You

Principle #33 - Men need to "*see*" in order to comprehend, meanwhile a woman needs to "*feel*".

A man will go into the store and purchase an entertainment center. One of those entertainment centers that needs to be assembled. Now the man "sees" exactly "what" he has purchased. He fully comprehends that he bought an entertainment center, which needs to be assembled.

Now when that man goes home, he opens up the box and sees all of these screws, nuts, different size boards, and glasses. Now instead of assembling the entertainment center using the detailed instruction manual, which is the **"why"**, he'll look at the box cover and assemble the entertainment center based on the picture of the finished product, which is the **"what"**.

I think the major misunderstanding in men and women relationships is very simple. I think the woman wants to know "*why*" he did this, said that, or "*why*" he isn't doing or saying something. On the flip side, the man wants to know "*what*" differences does it all make (ha, ha). Remember men are not that big on detail. So the little specifics that are important to you as a woman, are a pain in the ass to a man. (Trust me sweetheart)

A man might not understand that how he leaves the house (very rudely) in the morning, is going to affect how you feel later on that night when he wants some loving. A man, either sees the **big picture** or the **only picture**. That's why a man can sleep with a woman and think nothing of it. It's easy for us to **only** see sex, as sex.

A man wants to see the bottom line. He really doesn't care about, who was there, where they came from, how they felt, and so on. So word to the wise: If you want your man to hear or "see" what it is that you're saying, show him the big picture or show him a picture. Don't give him a bunch of details or adjectives. The bottom line will do just fine. Show him the "*what*", and he'll get it immediately.

Men are not insensitive like many women are lead to

believe. It's just if you start to give a man too much detail, he'll be out to lunch (thinking about sex, money, or the game), while you're talking. Giving a man too much detail will cause him to cut you off, losing interest and focus.

I'll share another little secret with you babygirl. Now this one you can't tell the fellas that I told you, okay. If you really want to dress seductively or sexy, this is what you do. Reveal that you have a body (establish that your body is banging), but just don't disclose your detail. That's it. That is all you have to do. Do you get it?

It's cool to wear something sexy. Just don't have all of your ass hanging out. Wear something nicely fit but not exposing your bare chest. Leave a little something for the imagination. Let a man see the big picture but leave your details for later (If he's worthy). Have you noticed that strippers start out wearing a seductive outfit, to get a man's imagination to working? Then, she'll undress and reveal her detail, only after a man is worthy (Gives her money). Think about that for a second, you can learn alot from a strippers seductive tactics.

Some of you ladies give up all your detail way too easily. Trust me it drives men crazy to see your sexy body (your what), but have to think about your detail (why). See how good I am to you. I'm telling you the things us men talk about in the locker room or in the park. Men are not that difficult or complex. So don't try to confuse us with unnecessary information and expressions.

The key thing to remember about your man or a man is that he **thinks** like a man. A man might not see things the way your mother, sisters, and girlfriends see them. A man might not see what you see. Consequently, he may not feel the same way you feel about something.

He is a **man** not a **woman**. Keep in mind that he is only thinking (the "what"), like a man. And he still loves you babygirl. So learn to respect and accept his point of view. It will only enhance the one you have already.

DivaGirl - How To Have A Good Man Find You

A Man Acts Like A Man

Nothing turns me off faster than an overly sensitive, extremely emotional, and feminine man. I can't stand a "soft" dude. And no, I'm not on that "macho man, real men don't cry" tip. It just bothers me when I see men acting like women.

$ Million Dollar Question
■ Acting like a woman? What do you mean acting like a woman? What does a woman act like?

$100 Million Dollar Answer
■ Are you serious? You mean to tell me that you don't know the difference between a man's and a woman's behavior? Well let me give you a little checklist.

Check Your Man

■ If he has more mood swings than you (check him)

■ If he's always whining (check him)

■ If he has no backbone (check him)

■ If he has more sass in his ass than you (check him)

■ If his braids and nails are neater and longer than yours (check yourself) ha, ha, ha, ha…

I could go on and on but I don't want to, nor do I need to. You know the difference between a man's and a woman's behavior (Don't play stupid). If you don't know then you better act like you know. There are a lot of men out here that are feminized. There are a lot of sweethearts, posing as men, passing on that HIV to you ladies. So be careful and use your better judgment. Don't let the muscles, durag, and the "fake thug" persona fool you. Every male ain't a man. (You feel me)

A lot of what I see today disgust me. I know all of the warriors, soldiers, and gentlemen of yesteryear, would be disappointed by the "chumps", "sissy's", and "suckers", we are breeding today.

Wisdom gem *- If a man acts like a man, it's because he is a man; If he is a man, he'll act like a man.

As a man, a man will do the things that men do. Within every culture there exist some social norms for male and female behavior. Therefore, I won't speak from a cultural perspective but a universal one. There are things that men do alike all over the world. It doesn't matter if a man is black, white, red, purple, or yellow, there are some things common to all men. Certain elements of life are indicative of manhood and maleness.

There are basically three things that influence a man's behavior. All men share a commonality in this life. We all must respect the same universal laws and principles. It's a fact that we all do different things and make different decisions with our lives. However, there are still three common elements of influence that affect every man's decision and action, regardless of where he is in life.

All men respond according to these three things. We may not all respond in the same fashion whether culturally or personally (personality), but we all respond to them.

Elements of Influence for a man
- Men need to establish their presence
- Men seek their private relaxation zone
- Men need healthy competition

DivaGirl - How To Have A Good Man Find You

Establishing His Presence

Has a man ever asked you, "who's is it", during sex? Do you think men ask that question because they want to own you? Not at all. Men ask that question because they are "trying" to establish their presence. Men are always doing things to establish their presence.

Men are always looking to settle into a position. Therefore, the man in your life wants to be the top dog. He wants to sit on the throne. When the ego gets involved, this natural tendency of a man can go from being something healthy, into something dangerous.

A man looking to establish his presence, is a natural occurrence for him as a man. A man looking to possess a woman, is dangerous and unnatural. So let me give you a little advice. Let me show you the difference between a man trying to establish his presence and a man trying to possess you.

If your man shows up at your job or house unexpectedly, he is "trying" to establish his presence in your world. If your man starts answering your phone, he is looking for the top spot. If a man says that you can't work, or go out with your girls he is "trying" to possess you.

Keep in mind men are very sensitive and positional creatures. It's only natural for a man to desire the top spot and seek to make his presence felt. I know that when I'm seeing a woman, I want to be the top dog (After her kids of course).

Wisdom gem* If you want your man to think he is your man, never put another man in front of him.

Now I want to talk about an innocent, little crime, many of you ladies commit on a regular basis when dealing with men. It is not beneficial for you to always talk about a baby father, ex boyfriend, male friend, or any other man, in the presence of *your man* on a regular basis.

The little, "Shawn is such a sweetheart", and the "Derek is

so funny", isn't a good thing when you're talking to **Jason**.

Wisdom gem* As a woman you're going to have to outclass your man. Until a man matures he is very egotistical.

      As the one that manages the relationship, you have to know how to stroke your man. That includes his ego, back, penis, etc… I'm not suggesting that you bow down to a man. We are talking about being wise with your man. It's in your best interest to let him establish a presence in your world, if he is your man. Then he will feel secure and know yours is a place he belongs. Remember, it "should" also work the same for you. If your "man" isn't given you any authority and say so in his world it can mean trouble. (Usually you're not his woman)
      Keep in mind you are always to exercise discernment and discretion with your decisions. Don't just let any man set up shop in your domain. Give it only to he that is worthy of having it (Your body, faithfulness, devotion, etc…).

A Little R & R

      Relaxation is important for everyone, especially for a performer…I mean especially for a man. Unlike a woman, who can relax in a group, a man needs some private time and space to unwind.

Wisdom gem* Ladies, ladies, my sexy ladies, if your man doesn't come straight home after work, it's because you are a pain in the ass. He may love you... *but you can still be a pain in his ass* (I can't stop laughing).

      A man needs silence, like a woman needs a hug. If he can't get that at home, he will look for it in the world. There is nothing more irritating for a man than to walk in the door, to a talkative, "I need you to…" demanding woman. Trust me, your man wants to help around the house. He wants to know "what" happened in your day. He wants to play with the kids and take them off of your hands. Just give the man a few seconds to get his mind right.

Remember men are performance oriented. Before he can go into the "husband", "boyfriend", or "daddy" role he needs to readjust his frame of mind.

When a man is watching the game in the living room all by himself, screaming at the television, he's actually relaxing. So don't assume because he's yelling at the television that he feels like talking about what happened to your sister in her relationship. If a man is relaxing and you come into the room with the "why, how, and where" conversation, he really doesn't want to hear it. It doesn't matter how important it is to **you**, at that moment it isn't important to **him**.

$Million Dollar Question
- So are you telling me not to disturb him when he's watching the game or when he comes into the house?

$Billion Dollar Answer
- That is exactly what I'm saying.

Most of the time in life in order to get what you want you'll have to satisfy someone's "wants" first. If you want your man to help out with the kids: Give him twenty minutes alone when he first walks in. If you want to talk to your man while he's watching the game: Tell him that after the game, you would like to share something with him. Trust me divagirl, that will work a hundred times better than starting an argument or catching an attitude.

Now if your man is one of these "all day video game playing, all night internet surfing" chumps, tell him that Rich will spend some time with you, if he won't. Then go into another room and read one of my other books. He'll never know what you're talking about. But I bet his ass will drop that controller and turn that computer off... pronto.

Understand how important a man's private time and space

is to him. It is sacred and holy to him. Give the man a couple of minutes and a few inches to do his own thing….. by **HIMSELF**. Just because he's watching television while you would rather talk, that doesn't mean he doesn't care about what you have to say. So there is no need for you to get your panties and bra into a bunch.

Now, if all he does is watch television and doesn't want to be bothered: He might not be the man you want to be in a relationship with. The bottom line is your man needs some private time and space to think and relax. If you give him what he needs, he'll be more willing to give you what you need.

Competition

Every man needs a little healthy competition in his life. You can call it "playing", or "boys being boys" if you like. But whatever you call it, a man needs it. When a man goes out to "play" ball like he's still a kid that doesn't mean he is not a man. Every man has a competitive side to him that he seeks to satisfy.

Men compete and measure themselves against other men. If Paul drives an Altima, and Tom drives a Benz, there is a strong possibility that Tom might think he's beating Paul.. Now how do you think Tom would feel, if he pulled up at the light in his Benz, but I rolled up next to him in my Bentley (I don't own one **yet**)? Exactly, he might then feel that he's losing.

Competition isn't a bad thing when it's kept within reasonable boundaries. That's why in all sports they have rules of competition to keep things fair.

Wisdom gem* Men don't like competing against women because men fear losing to a woman.

A confrontational and competitive woman, feels like a threat to a competitive man's sense of manhood. A man can handle losing to another man. Losing to a woman will rub him the wrong way. You don't have to agree with it or believe in it, but men are not trying to compete with women. It doesn't matter if he is competitive or not.

Have you noticed that many men can't handle their woman making more money than they do? Have you noticed that men try to keep women on the sidelines, as spectators? I'm telling you, a man's competitive nature is satisfied best, when he's competing against another man. With that in mind, a woman that loves to "debate", "win every argument", or prove her "righteousness" all of the time can become annoying within a relationship for a man.

So understand a man needs a little healthy competition in his life. So let him go out and "play" with the boys. Let him hang out with the fellas. Never forget that your man really doesn't want to fight, battle, and go to war with you.

As a woman, you are a man's soft spot. Men love femininity and class. The fussing and fighting he expects and accepts from the world. From his woman he wants support, nurturing, and some sweet loving. So if you're competitive, join forces with your man, become his teammate and not his opponent. Compete with him and not against him.

A Man's Love

Have you ever been in love with a man that was in love with you back (Sounds like a song)? How did you know that he loved you? Did he do the same things for you that you did for him? I bet his love manifested in a slightly different fashion than your love for him did.

It always bothers me when I'm in a relationship and a woman says, "she loves me more than I love her". How ridiculous of a statement is that, if love is love? A man manifests his love in the world differently than a woman manifest her love. God is love. Meanwhile, men and women represent different dimensions of God in the earth. Therefore, men and women both love. We just do so differently.

Often times a woman will think that her man doesn't love

her, or that she loves him more because her love manifestation may be more affectionate, emotional, and verbal. Don't be misguided into believing a man's love isn't strong because he doesn't express it like you do.

It's a fact that many men today are poor at expressing themselves emotionally to a woman. Men assume that because something is clear to him, (He sees the big picture) that the woman will also see what he sees. Like I stated earlier, men and women communicate differently. So expect for him to express his love in other ways than you do.

There is no such thing as, "I love you more than you love me". As long as there is only one God, then there is only one love. A man's love manifests in more mental ways than emotional manners. A man may only have to think a loving thought towards his woman to be satisfied: Meanwhile his woman may need to hear loving words.

A man loves with a strength and power that is different than a woman's love. Men want to direct and protect that which they love. While a woman may want to correct and nurture what she loves. A man will do whatever he has to do to insure that his love is taken care of physically (shelter, clothes, cars, etc…), but might neglect his love emotionally (affection, conversation, etc…)

Babygirl I hope you understand that a man may not express his love for you, in the ways you do for him. But he still loves you. He may not be as good with words or with his soft emotions as you are. But he still loves you. A man loves like a man, because he is a man. A man doesn't love as a woman, because he isn't a woman.

Raising The Bar

I've already addressed the misconception of Mr. Ideal. I've already spoken to those of you ladies that need to humble yourselves and lighten up. We understand that some of you need to give up that "bitchy" and "I'm all of that" attitude.

Now, it's time that I speak to those of you ladies that are

allowing men to just say and do anything. It's time to address those of you that are cosigning on a man's "bullshit".

Letting a man be a man is a positive thing. Don't misunderstand where I'm coming from. Usually when someone hears that "boys will always be boys" or "he's only being a man", it's immediately associated with a negative behavior. What I'm talking about is allowing a man to be what he naturally seeks to become and express.

I have a bone to pick with some of you ladies. For those of you who allow men to get away with murder, we need to talk. For those of you who are easily impressed by the "shinny" things, I need to holla at y'all for a second. It is time to **raise the bar**.

I personally feel that the current expectation level for men is way too low, especially for African American men. If you think that a brother is all of that just because he isn't in jail, **raise the bar**. If you allow a man to cheat on you just because he is good looking and has money, **raise the bar.**

If you are the other woman (he's married, already has a woman), **raise the bar**. If you think Jeff is the "right man", just because he puts it on you in the bedroom, **raise the bar**. If a man has no ambition or direction and you allow him to live off of you, just to say that you "have a man", **raise the bar.**

Let a man be a man. Some of you ladies are making it too easy and convenient for men to be trifling. Do you realize if you support or applaud a man's "half ass" ways and behavior, you're cosigning on a bad deal?

When you accept his unfaithfulness, you're just as guilty as he is. When you stick around for the second, third, and forth ass whuppin`, you are basically asking for it (I had to say it).

For those of you ladies that are currently in abusive relationships, I have some advice for you. Pick yourself up, and go into the mirror. Just stand there looking into your own eyes. Then ask yourself these three simple questions.

    *   "Do I value the person that I see?"

    *   "Do I want to improve this situation that I am in?"

      *   "What step can I take right now that will move me forward?"

      If you asked yourself those questions, now look yourself in the eyes until you are satisfied with your answers. There are too many women allowing these punk ass males to put their hands on them. There are plenty of domestic violence programs in your white/yellow pages that will assist you in moving forward. If need be you can also email me. I'll shine whatever light I have onto your situation to help you out. Keep in mind, I'm not a "know it all" or doctor of any sort.

      Letting a man be a man is about letting the God in him manifest. If you ladies continue to allow some men to get away with "being" and "doing" wrong then they will never get it right.

Principle #35 – Until a thing is proven wrong, it will continue to exist as if it's right.

      Let that man know that you want "a one woman man." Let that man know that there will be no physical altercations going on with you. Never ever let a man walk on top or beneath you. A man is to be by your side or a little ahead of you. Make it clear to Mr. Man that his mind has to be right, before he can get with you.

      If you are working and making it happen, let him know he also has to <u>bring</u> it. If you're at home building a family, let him know that he has to invest into his family as well.

      Raise the bar. We are all capable of one hundred times more than we are currently showing. So as you begin to walk in the greater dimensions of life realizing more as a woman. As you are maximizing your womanhood, and walking in your purpose: Make sure you are doing two important things with Mr. Lover.

- Let him be a man (the man) in the relationship.
- Inspire and expect greatness (raise the bar) out of him.

A man that is challenged by an awesome woman will only do one of two things. He will run from the relationship and "pressure" that you apply to his manhood, or he'll step up and accept your challenge. Always remember, a real man will embrace his manhood and purpose. A real man will appreciate you more as a woman, if you inspire him to be more in this life. Trust me on that divagirl.

CONCLUSION

This chapter was written to help you better understand your man's world. I wrote this chapter so that all of you single ladies out there would gain more insight into a man's psyche. When I say, "let him be a man" I'm not implying that you allow him to cheat on you, or to walk all over you as a woman. I am suggesting that you allow his natural tendencies and nature to express itself freely. I am recommending that you raise the bar.

A man is a beautiful creation of God, just like you are as a woman. Too many women have allowed their men to become "suckers", "punks", and "cowards". Remember, Eve was there to improve the situation, not to make it a bad situation. I feel that too many African American women have made it easy for our African American male soldiers, husbands, fathers, and sons, to become "niggas".

Kick your man, your son, your brother, and your husband in the ass, if you have to. Get the best out of him. Be one of the main reasons why that man will be all the man he can be in this life. Let him know that you expect nothing less than a man from him.

Trust me, if you become that inspiring force in a man's life, he will love you with all that he is. Many mothers are the inspiration behind their sons, but you can also be one as a wife, girlfriend, fiancée', sister, etc…

As I close I want to leave you with some practical advice: A lot of you women seek advice about men or about your man from other sources, mainly other women. If you're not safe, that advice will soon become techniques and strategies. Don't play games **against** your man (manipulate, coerce) play **with** him (cooperate). That man needs to be a man. Stop trying to conform him into a woman.

If it's a woman you need, call your mother, call your girl Pam, or call that sissy Raul from the salon. Let your man, be a man. As a woman you will naturally influence certain changes and developments in a man's life. Just keep in mind, he will never be you. Your man will never be the woman you may want him to be. So expect to disagree, misunderstand, and to "not know" from time to time.

Expect your man's world to compliment yours as a woman. Men need to be challenged. It's important that you have a standard about yourself. Never allow a man to think, it's cool for him to play video games all day. Don't let that man think every thing is "ire" (Jamaican accent), as you bust your ass everyday, paying all of the bills by yourself.

And if that man puts his dirty hands on you, leave him,. right after you make him piss blood for a week. Let him be a man. Keep that bar up high, no *excuses*. Let that man be a **MAN**

CHAPTER 11

Why Men Marry: The Real Reason

"I want to get married… BUT I need to finish school first, I need to make more money, weddings are expensive, my divorce ain't finalized yet, I want to wait a couple more years, marriage ain't what it use to be, my parent's divorce really devastated me, we're moving too fast, I'm afraid of hurting you………"
Some of a man's reasons for not getting married

INTRODUCTION

Now here is where the getting gets good. **WHY MEN MARRY?** Just think about that question for a minute. Better yet, why don't you answer it for me?

Billion Dollar Question
- **Why do men get married?**

Trillion Dollar Answer
- **(Your answer here)**

If you really think about it, this is the question you've been trying to answer in all of your relationships, thus far. You've been cooking, cleaning, sucking, humping, and doing everything you've been taught, trying to answer the question (Will he marry me?) You've called the radio station seeking advice. You've purchased books and magazines looking for answers. You've even taken your ass to church, praying to God for a breakthrough. Yet somehow none of that seemed to work for you. The advice you received from that radio personality didn't work, because he/she didn't know shit about your situation and relationship (but the little you told them), but they told you what to do anyway. All of the books and magazines you read give you a bunch of "text book" theories, but you live in a "real world" where things need to be practical in order to work. Your prayers haven't been answered, because you pray without faith and you don't know God's Will. So what now? What's your next step babygirl? You're now ready to just give up because you think there is no answer, right? **WRONG!**

Contrary to how things may appear today, men are still marrying women. In fact, people get married everyday some got married today (It could have been you). And contrary to popular belief, "most" men *do* want to get married. **BUT,** men marry for a reason. Men marry for a special purpose.

So being the man that I am, I will deliver what I promised. I'm gonna tell you, as well as show you, *why men marry*. So get ready because I'm about to take you there once more. You have to admit this book is pretty good, right babygirl?

Billion Dollar Question
- Why do men marry?

Priceless Answer
- Men marry because they *"see"* their wife.

See Their Wife?

That's right, you read it right. Men marry because they "see" their wife. Remember men are highly logical and visual creatures. So we need to "see" (vision) our way through life. Unlike a woman, who needs to "feel" her way. As a result, until a man "sees" his "wife", don't expect him to marry. Men need to "see" their way into marriage. And if he doesn't "see" his wife, you won't "<u>see</u>" him marrying. No matter how the woman may "feel" about the situation.

I can just hear you now: So what's a wife and who is she? Well for starters, a "wife" is only reserved for a woman. So all of you "girls", "mothers", "daughters", "bitches", and "ho's" reading, this ain't for you. (Sorry but I have to keep it real) A wife is a <u>woman</u> that possesses four super qualities that make her more than just a woman. A wife:

- ➢ She's a Friend
- ➢ She's a Lover
- ➢ She's a Business Partner
- ➢ She's a Role Model

She's A Friend

How many of you ladies know how to be a friend to your man? I mean how many of you would have a good time with your man, if you two were on a deserted island, with no radio, no T.V., no money, and you two couldn't have sex.

Friends enjoy each other's company regardless of the situation or circumstance. A wife is a friend because she can have a good time with her man, anytime and everywhere. As a "friend", a wife represents "fun" to her man. And all men love to have fun. If your man has to leave your company before he can have fun, it will be a cold day in hell before he marries you. So to all you stiff, "head in your ass", bourgeoisie females, *loosen up*. Leave all of the "professionalism" out in the world and have fun with your man.

Keep it real, who wants to commit to a lifetime of boredom. If you and your man don't play, laugh, and have a genuine good time, forget about marriage babydoll. Men marry the woman that is their friend.

DivaGirl - How To Have A Good Man Find You

She's A Lover

Sex is a big thing in theory but a small thing in application. Of the 168 hours in a week, how many hours are you actually having sex? Now I don't care how sexual a being you are, I doubt if more than 10% of your time (16.8 hours of the week) is spent having sex. Unless of course you make your living by lying on your back. (Some ladies do)

Now with that in mind, I hope you realize that you can be a lover to your man 24/7, 365 days of the year. How you speak to your man, how you look at your man, how you touch him can all be in a loving manner. Many women mistake the nurturing of a mother, with the loving of a woman (wife). A wife doesn't baby her man like a mother, but he still feels secure and cared for in her presence. A wife doesn't provide for her man like a mother, but he's taken "*care*" of by her.

As a "lover", a wife represents "care" to her man. If your man doesn't feel that he is cared for, why would he care about marrying you? I think too many of you ladies underestimate the power of "care" and overestimate the impact of "sex" on a man. (I said a MAN). A wife is a "lover" because she cares for her man. Men marry the woman that is loving, the woman that genuinely *cares* for him. So to all you with the "I don't give a fuck" attitude, expect a man to feel the same way about you. I don't care how "pretty" you may think you are, you are not above treating a man with care.

She's A Business Partner

People often overlook the importance of "work" to a relationship. For some reason we just expect things to happen. When a man and a wo-man come together, a greater man is created. One of the reasons for man being on earth is to accomplish, achieve, and advance out in the world. A wife is a business partner because she "*works*" with her man, as an equal partner, to bring accomplishment and achievement into their lives and into the relationship.

If you've ever really been in a relationship (forget a marriage), you know that "work" is required if things are going to work. And if you've ever accomplished anything in life (we all have), then you understand that "work" is a prerequisite of achievement. Now with that being said, a wife is a business partner to her man (husband) because she multiplies and manages with him. She helps to multiply and manage whatever *they* "work" to create (Family, wealth, success, etc)

As a "business partner", a wife represents "help" to her man. Remember Adam **needed** a helpmate. So if your man feels that you're a "hindrance" instead of a "help" to his progress in life, you can cancel your Christmas and all plans of marriage. If a man is making moves or has goals and a vision, why would he want someone to slow him down?

To all my sexy ladies dealing with African American men, the last thing that man needs is another obstacle in his life. The last thing he needs is a woman to hinder his progress. He **NEEDS** help and a man marries the woman that will help him. So let's start multiplying the good and subtracting the bad in your man.

She's A Role Model

Unfortunately, society has conditioned men to undervalue the worth of the **WOMAN**. Men have been taught to look at the woman as a piece of property, as a piece of ass, or as a pain in the ass. As a result, the woman isn't a role model to every male. But to the man, a wife is a role model because she inspires her man to become a better human being. A wife teaches and strengthens the human qualities (faith, love, hope, etc.) in her man, similar to that of a mother.

Just like a man appreciates and adores his mother, so a man appreciates and adores his wife. Unlike a mother who inspires her son from boyhood into manhood, a wife inspires her man from manhood into Godlikeness. A mother inspires here son to be a man, but a wife inspires here husband to be a God (Godlike). It's because of his wife that a man becomes a better person on the inside and out.

As a "role model", a wife represents "growth" to her man. A man marries the woman he knows that makes him a better person. So if your man feels like all you do is tear him down (with insults, complaints, etc), he's not marrying you. Why would he commit to a lifetime of depression and degradation?

A wife is a role model because of the virtue and value she brings to her man makes him more as man. She brings out the best in him and he realizes more in this life because of her. So to all of you "negative, nasty acting" women, understand that you are not a Godly model or teacher of Godlikeness.

Pay Attention

So as you can see a wife ain't no joke. Not everything soft and pink qualifies as a wife. Not every woman makes the cut. So for all of you aspiring wives, read this chapter again and again, until something goes off. There is a hidden message within this chapter...and once you find it...***BINGO!***

The woman (wife) I just described will have men running to the altar instead of having men running away from it, unlike many of you women today. Right now men are not that quick to marry because they don't _see_ their wife in their women, and marriage _**looks**_ (remember we "see") like a dead end street (like death). And what person in their rational mind is looking forward to a dead end, or hopeless conclusion. How many people do you know that are looking forward to death? Exactly, so until a man _sees_ a wife, marriage will look like death. Now why would he want to die...I mean marry?

Men & Marriage (Right VS Wrong)

So now that I've showed you what a wife is, let me show you the right and the wrong way men go into a marriage. A man will marry under two circumstances and situations. One of them is the right way and the other is the wrong way, in my opinion. And these two circumstances are:

1. A man finds a wife.
2. A man settles for marriage.

Finding a wife and settling for marriage are as different as night and day, and are as right and wrong as true and false. Whether you want to hear it or not, there is a right and a wrong way for a man to marry.

I'm finding that so many of you women are so set on "being married", that whether a man is marrying you for the right or wrong reason doesn't seem to matter. It seems like, as long as a man puts a ring on your finger, then it must all be good, right? **WRONG!**

A man <u>asking,</u> "Will you marry me?" and a man <u>saying</u>, "Let's get married" are the difference between life and death to a marriage. Now let me explain.

Will You Marry Me? (Right Way)

The bible says that, "he who *finds* a wife, *finds* a good thing". To me, this is one of the many verses of scripture found in the bible that is misused and abused. Preachers are preaching this, women are proclaiming it, but too many men don't believe in it (like many other things in the bible). A "wife", based on the definition and description I gave, is something special. To me she is not the "average, everyday" female, I hear and see nowadays.

I'm sorry to admit it, but not only is today's man "half-assed" but so is today's woman. (That's right I said it) So for a man, finding a wife ain't as easy as many of you women would like to believe. For a man to <u>see</u> someone that is fun, who cares, who helps him, and who makes him better, all in one women, is **special**. That women isn't every woman. That's why I think most men today are settling for marriage, instead of finding and marrying their wife.

Men choose to marry the "all purpose" woman that "homey, lover, friend" type of woman. And once he finds her, it doesn't take him years to recognize it. (Trust me I know!) Once a man finds his wife, he will want to marry her immediately, as long as his mind and money are right (He's stable). If his money is funny, then time will be an issue, but only because of financial reasons. Not because of the woman.

So when a man asks for a woman's hand in marriage and it's by choice (he sees his wife) and not because of circumstances, he is marrying for the right reason. When a man proactively chooses to be in a situation, it's because his passion, ambition, and values are in agreement. As a result, he is in the best possible position for responsibility. So a man choosing to marry a woman is a good look for that marriage.

If I were a woman, I would only want to marry the man who "chose" me as his wife.

Let's Get Married (Wrong Way)

When a man settles for marriage, it's usually because the *circumstances* and not the woman are the cause. Children, years invested into a relationship, the "pressures" of "should", and many other circumstances are leading men to marry today. As a result, men are marrying, but unfortunately many are not marrying their wife. And in my opinion that is the wrong way to marry.

If you desire a loving husband, let him choose to marry you (will you marry me). Don't try to use the circumstances of life and y'all's relationship as justification. If you do you're asking for a potential problem (I want a divorce).

DivaGirl - How To Have A Good Man Find You

Wisdom Gem*: Men marry their wife not the circumstances of life or a relationship.

Marrying for a green card, marrying because someone is about to do a jail sentence, marrying because y'all have forty kids together, or marrying because y'all been together for a hundred years, is still not the right reason to marry.

As a woman, once you become a wife (a lover, a friend, a business partner, a role model) to your <u>man,</u> marriage is inevitable. Therefore, don't settle for marriage just because you think you're getting old, or because you have multiple children. Marry for the right reason. Men marry because they *"see"* their wife.

"Let's get married" is a good idea and in many cases seems like something you "should" do, but men don't commit to good ideas. Men commit to purpose. Remember men marry for a reason.

<u>CONCLUSION</u>

So there you have it in a nutshell. Men marry because they *see* their wife in a woman. How pretty a woman is, her nationality, and all of the other cosmetic elements are factors in a man's marrying decision. But **seeing** his wife in a woman is the supreme reason. Remember, men are always looking for "that" (his Eve, his wife) woman. So as you can see there is an answer to that infamous question; why do men marry? So become a wife and be living proof of the answer. Can you handle that baby?

SPECIAL NOTE:

"Real Men Do Real Things" and "Punaney Galore" are hot novels that tell a vivid and entertaining story of this chapter and more.....................

I know that I keep promoting these other titles to you but they are truly "off the hook". They are a must read if you're reading this book.

CHAPTER 12

HE WILL FIND YOU

"He who finds a wife (good woman) finds what is good"
(Proverbs 18:22 NIV)

INTRODUCTION

So you've made it to the end of this book. Congratulate yourself for sticking through with it until the end. I've actually enjoyed writing this book. I've enjoyed being able to share with you some insight into manhood, womanhood, love, and life.

So far we've talked about being a lady, what men want, letting him be a man, and so on and so on. Now, I want to fill in the last piece of this beautiful puzzle we've been working on. At this point you're feeling good about yourself as a woman. You now honor what God has placed in you as a woman. The "bitch" and "ho" is dead. It's all good in the hood.

All there is among you now are beautiful women and lovely ladies. I'm so proud of you divagirl. Now you really really have it going on. Yet for all of the progress you've made so far, there is one thing missing. Remember the subtitle did say "how to have a good man find you" right? So where is the "good" (right) man.

Many of you that have actually taken some time to read this book, and who are applying its principles and advice: You ladies may already be on the "love train" heading to paradise. For those of you that ran through this book, like it were only for entertainment purposes, reread the book. This time apply whatever you think is relevant to your life. It's important that you do so. If not, this chapter in the book won't apply to you. If you don't apply the principles in this book this chapter is just some more "entertainment".

<u>You Are Different Now</u>

You are not the same woman now that you were at the beginning of this book. You may be the same size physically, live in the same quarters, and you may still have the same name. But you are different. I say that because I understand the power of exposure and principle.

Hopefully, many of you are now free from all of the "bullshit" that was binding you. I pray that you recognize being a woman and lady is an opportunity of honor. You realize that being yourself is a once in a lifetime blessing. Can you now see that men are not that bad after all?

I believe that you have a newfound respect and admiration for the purpose of God that resides in his male creation. You've forgiven your father, baby father, the man that molested you, and every other man from your past that rubbed you the wrong way.

You are free divagirl. I hope that you are smiling from ear to ear with that pretty smile. Never before have you had the opportunity to experience all of the good and perfect things that are coming your way. Trust, that your life is only improving in perfect ways. You are in the best position you have ever been in. Life will respond to you accordingly. Get ready because it's on now.

DivaGirl - How To Have A Good Man Find You

<u>Stay Connected</u>

My first objective with this book was to free you of all the "false things" that were living as truth in your world. I wanted to realign you back with the truth about men, women, relationships, and love. If I was the least bit successful then you are connected to the ultimate source of love, happiness, and success.

If you are operating on the truths and principles in this book then you are in the abundant flow of life. Expect men to step up and approach you from a respectable and mature angle now.

Expect to meet men that are handsome, intelligent, single, and going in your direction. Understand divagirl, that the world is yours. It's up to you what will be.

In spite of all the good you have going on: I still have one concern. I hope all the progress you've made, isn't short term or a temporary change in your life. I hope that if you have a disappointing experience it won't discourage you. I hope it won't bring you back to your old frame of mind. I hope that you often revisit some of the chapters. Allow this book's message to resonate in your spirit and soul. I pray that you stay connected.

Principle #37– The same thing it takes to obtain it also takes to maintain.

When you and Mr. Right hook up, don't forget that sex ain't love. When you two meet, remember the importance of romance and continuing to explore the depths of each other's souls. Never forget what men really want, even if he isn't asking for it. Stay connected to the truth.

Realize that some of your girls may try to throw "salt in your game". That's why I recommend that you buy them a copy of the book, lend it to them, or just encourage them to buy their own There is nothing worst than being the only one thriving in your circle. So spread the love and put your girls on.

Spreading the love will only increase the love and blessings in your life. Stay connected babygirl, grow and mature in the things we have covered in this book. You are a good woman. It's official now. So how does it feel special lady?

He's Looking For You

Do you realize that Mr. Right is looking for you, right now as you're reading this book? You do recognize that your man wants to do right by you and be an awesome man?

As a woman you don't have to force anything upon a man and here's why:

1. The masculine force in the world is always looking for it's feminine compliment.

2. Men are always looking for women.

3. A good man is magnetically attracted to a good woman.

Mr. Right is definitely looking for you. Therefore, you don't have to hunt Mr. Right down at the Knicks and Lakers game. You don't have to sashay yourself into VIP at the club, looking for Mr. Right. Your man is looking for you.

Mr. Ideal is never coming but Mr. Right is on his way. With that in mind, I hope you're now open minded enough to speak back to the man that approaches you politely. One never knows what a person may bring.

That brother who is always so nice to you in your building complex, might be Mr. Right. The guy your aunt has been insistent that you meet, might be Mr. Right. You never know, that dude you met on the Internet can be him. Understand that you are now free and the sky is the limit. Don't limit your possibility at how and where you must meet Mr. Right. Remain open minded and expect to meet him. Just let him reveal himself.

DivaGirl - How To Have A Good Man Find You

Take Your Time

Right now you are probably all excited and ready to make it happen. You want to meet Mr. Right and "find" love ASAP. Be careful that you don't allow your zeal to become impatience. Be patient at all times because what's yours is yours.

You don't have to start nagging your man to change. You don't have to chase every good looking brother down the street.

Just because you've read Divagirl and now have your mind right, doesn't mean you have to force your perspective or desires on other people.

All you really have to do is focus on yourself and grow as a woman. Remember, it's what you bring to the table and what you send out into the world that reflects what you experience. Don't allow arrogance to settle in as you become unreasonable with your expectations. Keep in mind even Mr. Right will do things wrong, disappoint you, and misunderstand your world from time to time.

So remain humble and let people grow in their own timing. Allow every man that steps to you to reveal himself and motivations. Have fun and date those individuals you find interesting. Do so without the "pressure" of "more". Invest the time to get to know someone before you give him the job with all of the company benefits. Let a man be a man.

For those of you ladies that have in the past been quick to jump into a relationship. For those of you that are quick to fall in and out of love. I have some sound advice that I would like to share.

Smart Advice

1. Sex comes easy. Sexual energy and attraction, is a natural thing between men and women. Never confuse a sexual attraction as something more.

2. It takes time to "really" get to know someone, even though there is always more to know. Conversation can reveal a person's intelligence and mentality. But one's character and beliefs are revealed by their actions. Give people the time and space, to reveal themselves.

3. If everything comes easy and is free for a man, he may not value it long term. Don't play games but make a man reveal his worthiness before you let him into your intimate territory. Don't open your door until you know who's knocking.

4. Have fun. Don't view being a single woman as a bad thing. Date, travel, meet people and learn more about yourself (intellectually, emotionally, sexually)

5. Go out dancing with your man or husband. Remember, relationships are opportunities. They are what you make them, nothing more nothing less.

CONCLUSION

Mr. Right is on his way. Your man will step up and become the man you inspire him to be. Divagirl, all you have to "do", is "be", the good woman and lovely lady that you are. I don't care if you are light skinned, dark skinned, White, Hispanic, or Asian, Mr. Right will find you.

It doesn't matter if you are petite, voluptuous, heavy set, tall, or short, Mr. Right is looking for you. Understand that you and Mr. Right's connection is more spiritual and of the soul, than it is physical. Therefore, Mr. Right may be a little shorter or taller than you prefer. Mr. Right may also be a few shades lighter or darker than the men that usually appeal to you. That is why you must remain open-minded, humble, and free.

Don't allow anyone's opinions, preferences, or beliefs to ensnare you. If Pam thinks your Mr. Right doesn't make enough money, that's her problem. She will be the first one smiling in your face when his business starts to boom and the money starts rolling in.

If your mother thinks your Mr. Right isn't any good because he's been in jail, that's her issue. She will be the first one to congratulate him, once he graduates from college and lands that nice job. Mr. Right fits you, that's why he's more than good. He's right. And trust me. Mr. Right will find you...

Conclusion

This was fun for me. I hope that you enjoyed the book like I did.. I really think that we need to do this again sometime in the future. I hope that I kept my word and challenged your beliefs, attitudes, and judgments. I truly believe that I have given you something different, and of value. I hope that you stay in touch and become a supporter of my efforts. May we do this again and again, and again and again............... (I look forward to it)

I really don't have a long articulate conclusion for you. I believe that I laid it all on the line throughout each chapter. I have given you all that I had to give (for now). I do have one more thing for you. There is one more thing we can do together that will fulfill this experience. I truly believe in the power of communication. And no form of communication is any more powerful than prayer. So let's end this experience on a powerful note.

Until the next book, love yourself, be yourself, and live the best life you can.......... Rich Gilmore

"Lord I thank you for the gift of life and for the power of womanhood. I'm a woman made by your hands and according to your purpose. With your direction and guidance I will express all that you have knowingly placed in me for your satisfaction. I realize that I am more than I've been showing. I am worthy of your best for me. I stand here making a new commitment to my womanhood, to love, and to living my life with purpose and value. Grant me the wisdom to make decisions, the love to inspire my motivations, and the humility to walk in my best. According to your perfect purpose in me."

**AMEN
DIVAGIRL...**

THANK YOU FOR READING

HERE'S MORE...

DivaGirl - How To Have A Good Man Find You

Real Book Series
Chapter I

The Sexiest Story Ever Told...

RICH GILMORE

- ■ What happens to young, good looking, rich, and successful men as they live the "playa" lifestyle in the city that never sleeps?
- ■ What do men do when they mistake lust for love and just can't say "no" to a big butt and smile?
- ■ What is the true cost of being a "playboy" in the game of love?

…..Finally there's a story that will answer those questions and tell the real hardcore truth about how men and women really get down.

Punaney Galore is the most explicit and scintilating story on how men lust, live, and love. It's a provocative tale of the three successful friends Denali, Akil, and Yes. It tells their stories as men, revealing the things they do and the lessons they learn, as they find love in a big city full of pretty women, sexy curves, and fast nights.

"This book is a definite page turner. It's a story for the fellas and for all the sexy ladies. I promise that you'll find yourself in the story and fall in love with the characters. Punaney Galore is sure to become an Urban Classic."

> Author's Guarantee
> Rich Gilmore

$13.95

Real Book Series
Chapter II

Real Men

Do

Real Things

How Real Men Get Down...

RICH GILMORE

Real Men Do Real Things

- What happens when the world judges a man by his cover but he's not what is advertised?
- What happens when people throw caution to the wind and follow their hearts in love?
- What really defines a man?

…. Well here is an authentic story that answers those questions and tells the real to real about manhood, love, relationships, and life.

Real Men do Real Things is the first provocative tale of its kind. It tells the story of what happens when the "elements" of the "church" meets the reality of the "corner". It reveals the real side of what happens when the cameras and lights go off and a man has to be a man. It shows a woman's perspective in the "transition" of love. This story cuts no corners, it tells the truth about how it "really" is out here in the world and not how it "should" be.

"This story is for any and everyone from the church, to the club, to the street corner. The characters Newman, Cybil, and Isaiah are people who you'll know all too well. I promise that you'll laugh, think, and feel good because of this story"

Author's Guarantee
Rich Gilmore

$13.95

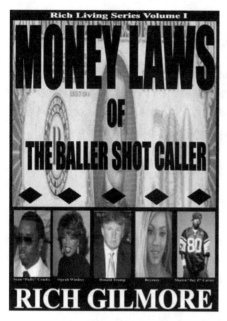

COMING SOON

RICH PUBLICATIONS is committed to being the #1 Urban Publishing Family in the industry. Bringing what's real and relevant to you the reader. We strongly encourage that you support our current & future projects because we are doing it all for YOU.

Upcoming Releases: By Rich Gilmore

Real Book Series Chapter III
"Sex, Money, Drugs, & Consequence" (2005)
The Realist Story Ever Told   **(Part I)**

"Certified Manhood" (Manhood Empowerment Series Volume I)
How To Be The Man In The Game Of Life

Real Book Series Chapter IV
"Crazy & Deranged"

Future Projects

Sex, Money, Drugs, & Consequence (The DVD Documentary)
A RICH FILMS PRODUCTION (2005)

Punaney Galore The Movie
A RICH FILMS PRODUCTION

For more info log onto: **www.richpublications.com**

About the Author

RICH GILMORE (27), Author & Entrepreneur

Rich Gilmore is the Founder and President of RICH ENTERPRISES Inc. which is the parent company of Rich Publications LLC, Rich Films, and Rich Entertainment.

Rich was born and raised in New York City but currently resides in the Northern New Jersey area with his wife Tanisha.

To contact Rich Gilmore for a book signing, speaking engagement or special event: Or if you would like to ask a question and/or make a comment, Email Rich at:

Rich@RichPublications.com

Or Mail To:
Rich Gilmore
P.O.Box 118
Lyndhurst, NJ 07071
Phone (888) 623-1800 Ext1
Fax (201) 842-0477

MORE DIVA SERIES

COMING AT YOU SOON

STAY TUNED... WE'RE FOCUSED

RICH PUBLICATIONS LLC is always looking for new authors, freelance writers, public relations professionals, investors, and sales representatives to join its rapidly growing publishing family. If you're interested, feel free to contact Rich Gilmore via email immediately at: **rich@richpublications.com** or call Rich at (888) 623-1800 Ext1

**Visit Your Local Borders, Waldens, and Neighborhood
Bookstore To Purchase More Rich Gilmore Titles**